I WOULD RATHER NOT BELONG

PILLARS OF CHANGE

Shabazz A. Rah-Khem, Ph.D.

| Contents |

∞ Introduction

"The role of the artist is exactly the same as the role of the lover.
If I love you, I have to make you conscious of the things you don't
see."
—James Baldwin, The Creative Process (1962)

I don't consider myself an artist, though I harbor a deep love for humanity, which allows me to understand our oneness with the essences of all life. Still, when I think of an artist, I envision a pure creative who can stir the hearts, minds, and sometimes even the spirits of people through their craft. In contrast, anything I've shared in this book stems from lived experiences, study, and the striving to unpack my higher purpose in this world, as well as continuing to grow through my life experiences. Thus, I am no artist. I approach this in some ways similar to research from a personal perspective: to become a better me with each day, each interaction, each idea, each experience. It's analogous to when I first embarked upon my academic research journey at Case Western Reserve University. My Chair cautioned that attempting to boil the ocean of knowledge in a body of work demonstrated a lack of strategy. The suggested path was to take one glass at a time, boiling it through critical inquiry and research. Even then, this could become a lifetime journey to contribute to the larger body of knowledge. Such is life and the pursuit of one's Best Self and purpose, through one's experiences, thoughts, interactions, or shared moments.

This leads to how I generate topics or poems of expression to write about. It's multifaceted: experiences (lived, past and present), people I've interacted with, questions posed directly to me from a network of people, things I've read (posts, books, articles, research papers), and/or music, that spark a thought of inner perspective that I decide to express, consider, examine, or address. Some of my thoughts, ideas, and inspirations flow in during my routine of getting up at 3:30 AM, meditating, praying, and working out. And these thoughts or ideas will interrupt me in a way, requiring me to capture the initial line or two, so it doesn't completely disturb, then I can go back to what I was doing in the moment. Later, I'll circle back, focus on those lines, and just write raw until I get it out of my heart and head.

Writing is a part of my learning, development, and healing process. It's not to gain praise, set some trend, or get accolades. It was only after sharing a couple of pieces with some closer colleagues that I even started to consider what I was writing might, in some small way, touch or help another person. And as with anything, some people really dislike what I write or try to contrive knowing something about me...which is funny and aggravating at the same time. Someone trying to surmise me from a glimpse or eyedrop-sized aspect of my heart and spirit expressed through the confine of words, bound by moments of time. That's what they are in some respects: a moment, a flash of light providing a little deeper look at what stirs within the well of my soul. Still, my writings are only fractal facets of who I am. But when people attempt to surmise me by my writings, it just exposes some degree of entitlement cloaked in their false self-righteousness, thinking they know and can judge someone else while being disconnected from who they are deep down. My singular line for them: I'm working on my own stuff in this life, you worry about working on yours, jackleg. How about it?

In this same vein, oftentimes, people want to compare what I write about and my style of writing—or lack of style, depending on the person's perspective. Even more interesting are conversations I have had with people who use themselves as the measuring stick to critique my writing. They aren't wading in to give constructive feedback, helpful insight, or tips, but to share what they desire. They insist upon imposing their thought processes, use of words, and any other tedious details they can contrive. Then they leap forward extrapolating. Thus, I must somehow do and be the same.

That's where they lose me every time. Asking to talk to me about *my* writing yet imposing *their* constructs or thoughts of who *they* believe me to be. Communication, the exchange of ideas, is about finding common ground in "we" and "us," not you versus me. That's why I usually step back and listen because, once again, arrogance shifts us from mutual growth and sharing experiences or insights to being completely about *them*. And that's where we tend to fail in conversations and social media. Don't tell me, share with me, and if you cannot fathom that, I am not writing for you—I am writing for all the various versions of me, my younger me, my current me, my future me, and those with whom my humble words might reach through a common thread to inspire in some way.

Those of you who think the world is all about you, I am not writing for you nor to you. I am writing in the hopes of fostering deeper connections within a "we" that has been burdened by this world—its falsity, suppression, narrow and sterile standards, and senseless harm. Also, I am writing about the beauty expressed and shared, the embrace of life, nature, the universe, the strength of humanity, and a higher purpose, the essence of all life that resonates from the quiet place within each human's heart.

That is for those whom what I share might vibrate with. That's it. Those seeking a word or voice that resonates with a part of them unheard in the mainstream narrative. Those who are seeking something different, not commercialized, not fancy, not always so professionally polished, that came from the stoop, the block, an open field, behind walls, surrounded by gun towers and concrete, the shallows, and have hit the hard realities of life—a life geared in hustle, grinding away each day of life. And then realizing the true work must start within, being authentic and real, just genuine, raw, sincere, from the thoughtful depths of the heart to heal, grow, and share in a noble manner to uplift our collective humanity. One person shining a little of their light in the vast darkness of a world that ofttimes seems decoupled from compassion and higher principles while knowing within we are bound to a greater light in true humanity, which is love.

That's my writing style and writing purpose. It's not for everyone, nor am I trying to be for everyone. Because to be for everyone is to be for no one all at the same time. Too generic, too sanitized, too dominant culture, too mainstream, too indoctrinated, and too damn *not* me. If you cannot accept that, kick rocks and move along. All the things I've grappled with throughout my life, I've finally started growing to a point of strength and inner love—a point where I don't need affirmation from some self-appointed authority to qualify or quantify my heart, my spirit, my voice, my power, my gift and my purpose. I am trying to do what others have so graciously done for me: share, inspire, strike a spark, and impart knowledge, wisdom, and understanding; we all have it...that *light*. We just have to have the courage to tap in and bravely allow it to flow within and eventually express it outwardly.

Let's light up the world and universe, my friends. **Be a Pillar of Change**[1].

This short book is a primer to start conversations and/or introspection.

---

[1] https://pillarsofchange.org/

∞ Poems

| Rather Not Belong |

Navigating a world that constantly tells us we must be a certain way, look like this or that. A world with a mindset that only sees us through a narrowly fabricated lens, defines us by distortions, half-truths, backward tales and betrayals. A world that tells us: we do not belong.

We learn your rules. We play your trivial games. Yet, we do not belong. We contribute. We build. We invent. We create. Still, we do not belong. We embrace ideals. We call for humanity to rise to lofty plateaus. Yet, we do not belong.

We are met with ignorance. We are met with hate. We are met with violence. We are told we do not belong.

We have dreams of love. We call out as peaceful doves. With a sniper's bullet, we do not belong.

We champion laws, showing separate but not equal is flawed. Still, we do not belong. We tilled the land, worked on bended knee, sweat and tears flowed in disgraced tyranny. Until we bleed and plead, unable to breathe. And we do not belong.

We march. We sing songs, bludgeoned by batons. Still, we do not belong.

We are placed in strongholds, surrounded by weapons and bombs, and still, we do not belong.

We traverse systemic practices, procedures designed to exclude, even though we are able to elude, still we do not belong.

We challenge redlines, false principles of privilege and false concepts of being pure or closest to divine, demonstrate that humanity is all of one kind. Still, this we do not belong.

We call out double standards, hypocrisy, along with the fallacy that you are better or entitled to rule over me.... And still, we do not belong.

So, as we refuse to stay contained within boxes, prescribed for us. Still, we do not belong.

And, if that is the way it must be in order to be free...

Then I'd rather not belong.

∞

| **Know No Fear** |

Showing up fearless, despite our fears.

They are rattled by my ability to raise my hand, to question what I see...

they scoff at my belief, sharing rationale and reason should be clear for all to see...

they bristle at daring, there're no big U's and little Me's....

they seem confused, you see, when I pierce their eyes to see if they truly believe the lies, they tell upon me....

how fearless I must be, to challenge lies of slavery and segregation was your claimed favor to me. It is not that I am fearless; it is a fact I shall not let fear to rule over me...

in silence facing perpetuate lies they cast upon me, wanting me to accept it, you see...

not that I wish to die courageously, but I know with each lie, bits and pieces of humanity die within me...

so, I stand fearless before thee so my babies can see unceasing lies...will not subdue me...

the truth of the atrocities committed against folks who look like shades and variants of beautifully hued me... fear to me is to die complaint and not free from lies ruling over me.

∞

| Oceans |

My pain does not wash away at the shorelines.

Despite creative might, it only comes on like a blacklight highlighting cracks and crevasses from the wreckage of a soiled life.

Anguished thoughts, trying to topple the hate that hate wrought...such a vicious cycle in this life I've brought.

Lost in the oceans of my mind staring backward in a mirror of time. Then as I align thankful that death comes over living again a million times.

I am told Life is unfair, thus I should be thankful I get to live life here vs there. Deflections from despair, in areas I should care, like there and there.

As I stare, numbed inside lacking care, memories reflecting how I delivered degrees of despair, the cries of them I dare not share.

Prodigal, lost in life's undertow, finally hearkening to signs with every blow, to no longer waste time given by the Sublime.

As I stand staring in reversed time across blood-soaked shorelines, souls call out to me, to remind me, none shall see me for Me.

∞

| **Arrogance** |

Arrogance, a narrow lens does vex, distorting the world context. A single perspective can only be, where shadows dim all other light, so reality must not be. Turn day into night, wrong into right, ignorance rages with might.

No room for doubt, no space to grow, ignoring the depths it doesn't know. Dismissing life's complexity, the dynamics of heart and soul pressed to flesh.

Within our societal context, arrogance hinders our best, our ability to communicate or connect... eroding humanity to its depths.

Centuries hewed, this relentless mindset ensues, with every uncounted death.

Where wisdom fades, arrogance is the blade most played, becoming our cojoined burden and debt.

Whether it be we or thee, a collective it must be to set all of humanity free.

A universe unveiled our souls see through the veil.

As we flee the hate portrayed against others just because they be.

Will you not come along with me on this mission to set humanity free?!

∞

| My Land is Lush |

Roaming the barren lands seeking an oasis within desert sands...

a place where people are unkind to their fellow man due to shades of complexion flowing as sands...

rich we reflect, the soil of sustenance, body and spirit flourish with harvest, as they press for profit.

It will not always be, as the floods of truth shall nourish us once again, you see...

and all shall know the truth of those despised, as they marvel at the beauty of our textured thighs...

We shall be free, even in a land that held us in captivity—claimed, not free... These shackles cannot stop the mind from breaking free.

∞

| Warrior's Embrace |

A rock, shaped and cut by currents thrashing, tumultuous waves—an artistic beauty, a life engaged under God's gaze.

Not sitting behind comforted gates, fearful of lessons to be learned as life burns, rewards earned, through pains others spurned—gauntlet after gauntlet turned... born into the light from a stranger's breath, as thou walketh through valleys of death.

∞

| Be Strong |

Truth is elusive to those whose hearts are consumed by fear...

∞

| Blood of My Blood |

Triple life w/o

How do we encourage brothers to hold up their heads in a warrior's stead when multiple sentences guarantee life until dead?

We don't argue of whether they did what they did... because we both know we were rolling in that life unscared.

You see, a tale unsaid.... we know they did what they did. But even as a kid, should they be left amongst the undead?

Simply said, a youthful life led...or was it life that led to this result instead? It's not as simple as the prosecutor said...trial for multiple lives, they pled....

Yet, do the math—instead three goons roll up, demanding payment or be left dead.... You know we rolled instead, gambling against life, not scared...

Being they dared, left in a pool of grams and dread. Self-defense one might have said, but damn, we know the life we led, Still, as we play moments out in our heads, why choose to take the fall for all three dead...?

My brother refused to break bread...telling me live my life instead.... when it was all said... a choice between two kids...how could one brother agree to leave another amongst the dead? Because one brother had big dreams in his head while loving rolling hard against outcomes guaranteed at least one dead.

See, that life the two brothers led...yet divine providence was said...one should sidestep dread because no proof was led.

But now sit counting blessings instead while brothers count days amongst the undead.

Survivor's guilt about lust after bread, tempest of anguish in one's head for a life both brothers led...now one sits hand against head...sometimes wishing to be dead instead....

because playing it back in his head.... thy brother's life is dead. How can one get it right in systemic outcomes in my head when it was a life, we both led...?

differentiated instead, a simple toss of statistical coins to potentially not end up dead...have not both brothers sinned in life led...?

but one brother said, "Don't be stupid to wish oneself amongst undead.... due to a life once lived."

My, my, how can we get ahead when souls yearn to break bread.... rolling against a wall on mountain head...?

gun towers with fifty heads breaking free from penal colonies of undead. One day, free again, thy brother has said...then the true devils shall dread.

This poem is to my brothers in the hope we shall one day liberate the undead..... refusing sentences   of   triple   life   instead.   ∞

| Communication-Liberations |

Unlock thy tongue, speak thy truth free through an empowering melody for all of humanity. We shall be liberated, you shall see. My pain, my agony, my harmony, my plea, my aspiration, my desires, my joy, my love, and all things in the universe that be.... tramp along with thee, for one day We shall be totally liberated and damn certain free... ancestors dedicated their blood, sweat, and tears for thee... Almighty, We shall break free! And in this life, it will be.

∞

| Never Fail |

Failure, my steppingstone, my jewels and lessons learned. We churn and churn, toiling to earn, while failing to discern how to do better in this life that we yearn. We never fail, as long as we grow and learn. From mental death, Twelve jewels do we earn.

∞

| Hoisting Black Sails |

Whispers in flight shimmer across the mirthful waters of night, sweltering temperatures until birthed.

Let there be no lurking and twisting of souls. Step forward, foe, for the future's plight is not trite, nor shall it be driven by spite.

Though enemies strike, their might shall not dim the light. Our spirits laid bare, recompense and forgiveness shall prevail, our inner beauty guiding through hollowed hells.

Compassion and love for all humanity shall break the grip of hatred, and betrayal — this is our mission's tale across the ethers to tell, life is not a drunken spell.

Oh, my people, stand at the helm, navigating waves of betrayal. Blessings await, beyond a living hell, just beyond the darkest place, on horizons breaking the gate of foggy haze, the promise land lays.

We shall experience triumphant unimagined by narrow sighted and haughty foes. Blessed art thy sacrifice in this life, through all thy paths, one are many, *We all are chosen*.

∞

| Contain Not Thy Heart & Learn Thy Spirit |

Lest others attempt to etch thy path,

Learn thy depths through anguishing trials in thy path.

Do not waiver in conviction what's sincere to thy heart.

Precious is the journey of every soul in spite, absence and void of the light.

Many shall attempt to prescribe thy mission.

As a centerpiece for their delight.

Yet, they only conceive a singularity for thy life.

Do not divine thy heart with another. Save thy soul.

Walk beyond lust of mind, understand thy purpose!

is not shade but life coursing with beautiful expanse, courses unlaid.

Diverse is thy craft, fear birth thy wrath.

Thy exalted state is not amongst the shuck and jive, feeble scraps, accepting a place and space designated as chaff.

Cling to thy heart, intermingle with thy soul source.

Do not acquiesce for vanity's sake, succumbing to power or false embrace.

Gain thy enlightenment with each journey thy

trek lost in wilderness with each step.

Stand before thy helm, embrace ethers as they move upon watery deep, in and out of darkness keep.

Know thy vision for recompense. Know thy soul, so thy heart shall be kept.

∞

| **Mirror, Mirror** |

Mirror, mirror on the wall, why do I afflict such pain against all I see in form just as me?

As I gaze upon reflected shades of me, why do I smite those in the same conditions as me? Do I not see atrocities committed against all as we? Can I not see how others revel at demonstrated hate at people just like me?

Why do I partake in self-hate? Raised hand destroying me...raging against all like me? Can't I see beauty or salvation for thee or me?

Why do I jest with lies set to kill me, my brethren, my family tree? O' Lord, when shall I wake from tragedy, break mental shackles binding me? O' Lord, why can't I see love and salvation for those just like me...as we kneel on bended knee with a yoke as unfree?

When shall I understand I must first love me? Ultimately, we, the blackest mirrors I can see nothing other than me...

| My Butterfly |

My butterfly is greater than I.

A tale whispered across winds and trees. Lay down thy sword and take up my word in deeds, that thou mayest become a general in the grandest of armies...

As I survey the landscapes I have ravaged, fulfilling plans as summoned, I grapple with the allure of glories, and honorable deaths. I have wrestled demons to thy depths, both within and without...I have conquered devours, and broken free from the chains of my enemies, an alternate me...

I have approached insurmountable odds with the gleaming joy of conquest. I've prevailed in the face of eminent death, where others surrendered instead, my closest companions had written matters as conclusions of doom...dismissing what I would dare bring to bear. I have proven naysayers time and time again in error, trivial minds due to the falsities they bear....

But oh, how the lands lay in waste as I crusaded for my inner faith... nightmares plague me, legions of forgotten foes my heart now carries. Thus, it has come time to transform, a multidimensional tactician born... no longer forlorn.

Applying thy long-range vision slate, sight beyond immediate and present state, as others fail to contemplate sacrifices one must make for heaven's sake.

The time stands high, oh warriors come nigh, elevate thy blade on high. The capacity of current leadership is forbade. A new role has been foretold for warriors of old, former slave children who have grown bold. You shall achieve victories across in these same lands you were forced to walk as a beggar, hat in hand, based on a sharecropper's plan, as they gleefully paid with shifting sand, unable to be caught in thy hand.

It has come nigh to climb mountains once dreamed too glorious and high, a freedom string, we have grabbed hold, tugging on it so bold, all in an effort to raise humanity from lies that we have to wait for our heavens in the skies ... but the truth is within the lies, if we could just learn how to love one another as brethren on High.

Transcending mythical roles as jah's soul, it is time to be bold... stand in front of sun as the ancients foretold.... thy soul made whole... Based in the messages from prophets of old... no more my Children chasing of wishing wells or being held in jail cells, finally breaking the devil's spell... Crowns of Knowledge is where thy heart shall dwell.

Thy will be done.

∞

| My Folks Want to be Free |

Soulful folk, along a kaleidoscope of hope.

As I stare into the dynamics of being, seeing souls of a multitude of folks smiling back upon me. Smiles cresting beautiful faces, masking their pain from different places. Saying unto me: it must be different for thee due to thy proximity.

I ponder behind eye shades as an ethereal sage, thy reprise to the skies, wishing away so many lies to thy surprise. My position, my degree, credentials of alleged pedigree, nothing beyond facades one can see. Frightening fractions separating the majority from me.

You see, folks calmly like me, other folks barely tolerate that we be. Thy story, thy truth, a raw report, an account to liberate in some sort. Folks might seem audaciously free, or foley wasting potential before thee merely because of proximity to dominant society, that is what you see.

But I must tell, I stand as a shell, despised as well for my likeness shone in the wishing well from which brethren I swell, triggering others to repel. So, no, I pray tell, my likeness does not dispel the falsehoods they tell, springing from thy righteous well.

My labor I sell, for a distorted lofty place, a few degrees from where the masses mentally dwell.

My wages mere handcuffs, scraping as I must, to hold slightly a plus as I ride this prison bus, titles make me not free. Bitterness as I know it to be, merely a step or degree of trickery, due to my proximity you perceived I be above those who look just like me...it brings no glee a pedestal given by decree tokenism over thee. Yet, as time maybe, I stand before thee unempowered no more free, just as disenfranchised you must see, behind glided doors are cages for me. I am not free.

Another container cell, heart abeyance, another living hell a broader world shackled cell...yet, I refuse to give them my will nor submit to the lies they tell. Proximity provides no bail, just a glorified hell. I, too, refuse to fail, master works come from the ink of my spiritual well.

Oh Lord, we shall not fail. I pray for thy insightful divine will to aid bringing an end to the lies this world tells. Breaking free from the gallows the souls of my folks one day shall bail. Even though this be a social jail, it encodes my DNA as swill. I seek not social spells nor to compel more folks to eat slop and ignorance they sell.

I wish for free love stories to tell at some point a life lived well. Debate though they will of some far-off heaven or hell I see in this world it's another deceptive childhood story they do tell, robbing us by servitude, cajoled not to rebel, boots upon necks and captives in cells, reaping fruits of the world so they can sell.

See, they tell us wait upon fairytales, making mockery of thy hearts while thy are in a social cell, Hope sold down a wishing well, tormented mental hell.

We have survived ugliness and valleys of hell. Now is the time to break free from a mental cell, to finally join humanity's liberty bell, or continue to subsist in communities of dominant cultures in social hell.

| My Secret Whisper, in Prayer |

Surely, I turn myself to thee, oh Allah, striving to be upright to thee, the originator of the Essence of All life, and I am not of the polytheist.

Surely, my prayers and my sacrifice, my life and my death, are all for Allah, Lord of the worlds.

No associate has thee, and this I am commanded.

I am of those who strive to algin with thy will, thou art the King. There is no God but thee.

Thou art the Lord, and I am thy servant.

I have been greatly unjust to myself, and I confess my faults, so please grant me strength against all my faults, for none grants strength against faults but thee.

And guide me into the best of morals, for none grants strength to pursue the best morals but thee.

Turn away from me the evil and indecent morals, for none grants strength against evil and indecent morals but thee.

Oh, Allah, make me successful as I strive to manifest the truth of my heart and spirit.

Oh, Allah, bless me as I strive to manifest the truth of my heart and spirit.

King of Kings, Lord of All Lords, the Essence of All Life. Amon. ∞

| A Fist for Truth & Power |

Raise a Fist for Truth and Power.

People tell me I am too gruff, too rough, too blunt, too harsh... when I raise my gift.

People ask me, where is your tact? Where do you intend to track, or do I have thoughts of ever turning back...when I raise my gift refusing to join their pact.

People tell me, this is not how to act. My words and rhythms should be just fun facts... but I reply, it's their lies tryin' to blot out the sky. That's why I raise my gift to the sky.

People tell me that it is so, so complex, the distortion will vex... but not to me, when I raise my gift... it is clear as can be. If we break free and grasp a mentally high tower, we too can have power, we, too, shall be liberated within the hour, knowing truth and love is revolutionary Power.

As I raise my gift.

∞

| Life's Seasons |

Change is the water fomented of life,

Love is the sunlight that warms us through life,

Compassion nurtures our spirits against strife,

Truth gives us courage to rise, knowing love is
not off in the distant stars...

Our humanity is held behind lies and bars...

Until we break free knowing how to Love all of
humanity as one of Ours.

∞

| Oxygen to My Hate |

Inaction is bait, oxygen to my hate.

Simply because it's rainbows, I celebrate you allow oxygen to my hate,

Idle in debate, oxygen for my hate,

As you hesitate, think you can relate oxygen to my hate.

Claim my pain, yet you are oxygen to my hate.

Cosigning bills of late, oxygen to my hate.

Cutting ticker tape, you are oxygen to my hate.

As you pontificate, you are oxygen to my hate.

You say you'll stop them at the gate, you are oxygen to my hate.

Hollow promises to date, oxygen to my hate.

Save bullshit, it's too late, you are oxygen to my hate!

| **Pushing P** |

What are we doing?

Are we working to solve problems or serve them?

Perspective — are we approaching it differently?

Passion — move beyond feelings to stimulate action.

Philosophy — without application in the real world remains theory.

Perfectionism — waiting to get it right allows it to stay wrong.

Power — truth without being frozen by fear.

Progressive — moving beyond the status quo as a barrier.

Performance — results, not feelings nor hollow words

Potential — we can make it happen.

Protest — letting it be known by pushing back.

Pointed — firm and clear.

Provocative — inspiring radical change

Promote — in everything we do!

∞

| Shine, Baby, Shine |

Concealing the beauty of your heart and spirit is the greatest tragedy one's life can be, denying the strength of thy inner majesty. Lay down that fear to walk upright. Be forthright, no longer scared of things that go boom at night through the ignorance of that blue light.

∞

| The Gaps |

In our social dynamic,

Where freedom is denied, liberty not offered, and justice turns a blind eye. Strength as a nation shall not be prevalent. And greatness that they pontificate as such is a twisted lily of lust.

∞

| **Truth of Power** |

Power lies in the ability to inspire.

Power lies in the ability to uplift.

Power lies in the ability to mend that which has been trespassed.

Power lies in the ability to heal hearts.

Power lies in bringing people together in unity.

Power lies in dispelling ignorance with enlightenment.

Power lies in building pathways of inclusion.

Power lies in demonstrating compassion instead of harm.

Power lies in speaking the truth courageously to unite.

Power lies in overcoming fear.

Power lies in demonstrating love.

Power is not predicated upon lies...

Power resides within our collective humanity.

Power is meant to empower.

If only we could recognize the inherent humanity of all to *step into power.*

Take care, beloved.

∞

| Vibrating Essence |

The song of the universe starts in your soul, melodically vibrating your heart with rhythmic drumrolls, transcending to your thoughts, to the depths of the beauty one can behold.

Once you are ready, you shall sing your song to the truths of this world through crying out so loud and bold, actions and deeds the love ballad told to the multitudes shall unfold...

Sing, beautiful children, sing so Bold!

∞

| Wading through the Shallows |

Experiencing unfiltered.

Appreciation for splendor of stars requires walking through the deepest darkness experienced thus far. These moments feel expansive in depth, essence of all life is still left. Asking for salvation and being provided with an inner connection, an eternal light unchecked. Like flipping a switch, through thy radiance a vision of Light not seen yet. Deep breaths, deeper breath, with sweet and some sour mixed, exhaling fearful tremors becoming a self, I just met. Engulf in thy Power.

∞

| **When *They* Doubt You** |

Tap within You

They will not see you nor will *they* recognize the potential within you.

They have narrow vision, scope, range, and limited understanding beyond surface assumptions about you.

They live within their own mental and spiritual cages of rage.

They are on the sidelines judging, on the other side of tables doubting.

They were there before your birth.

They grimaced at your birth.

They strew barriers, pitfalls, closed doors more times than you care to remember.

They hoped you wouldn't survive the worst.

They can't conceive of your worth.

They have never been courageous; thus, *they* envy your courage.

They despise because you remind them that despite best efforts and lies you still rise.

They fiend as friend, yet covert actions are foe, my friend.

They have tried to extinguish your light, the dirt they do beyond the night.

They shall never understand you, nor should you care if *they* do.

They will not accept thy beauty, nor do they want you to.

They will always be just that...*them.*

You shall be you, no matter what *they* say or do.

Thy trials and tribulations, stumbles, fumbles, errors and deviations, lessons making you stronger.

That strength, resilience, intelligence, and power are the light of you,

What *they* don't know: each learning experience, small accomplishments, wins, silent successes, amplify your growth.

Raise thy head, child, open those radiant eyes and smile because *they* don't know true beauty as you do.

Don't sweat the *theys* of the world.

They have nothing on you.

They do what *they* do.... And still, you are beautiful, beautiful you.

Smile and know thy grace and power...because *they* don't know half thy story.

And it still grows, each day, with great glory. ∞

| White Lies |

Do you think I cannot see how you try to play through white lies?

You smile wide as a pie, but through every word and breath is a white lie.

You act so pious, remorseful with each die...just when you think they may catch you in the habits of a lie. Traits, behaviors that violate.... but there you go again, smiling. Oh my? Hand on your breast as you falsely cry.

No, no, I didn't mean to offend, as you pretend. I truly do consider all the colors of the spectrum and rim, my friend... and none is true, as you tell your white lies... as you always do!

How you don't see color as if it were true. While nothing more than a stylized white lie told by you...claiming to be good, never offending or hurtin' someone, twisting of truth as you do... because you be through and through claimed to be good too... So, so, good, as you do, telling your lily-white lies, as you do.

Yet, you work this system, through harmless snides, as if you would curl up and die.... But I know the truth of your little white lies. You liven such a big ol' lie... navigating this dominant world as you do, while claiming suffrage too...

But I know the truth about you. You are evil as you do, telling your little whites, as you screw me over through and through. Shape shifter, behind those doleful eyes, so full of lies. I truly know what's true... you hate us some much as you do, through and through.

Because the little white lie is truly you.

∞

| Playing the Part |

We claim legends and lore of wicked beasts, foul, awful monsters lurking beneath. Stories are told to young babes of how to be good little tykes, learning their manners and the like. We warn them of demonic behaviors dragging people into endless depths, unreturnable portals snatching of the innocent.

Internally, we wrestle with ravenous ravens and false doves, shedding thou armor to our souls, fumbling along, scared of fairytales from yore... what we do not seek, blood trails spring from the entrails, tales of betrayals retold, man's lust does unfold. No folktales be told, it is the evil of men tipping the scales as an alleged lady wears a blindfold.

The farce is larceny, untold in all thy stories of monsters so bold, yet it is not a beast nor demons feasting upon thy brethren's hearts and innards sevenfold... It's true hordes of men disguised in forked stories of old, we are sold. No more lies, no more lash and lace, no more alleged monsters from outer space...

The monsters are waiting in place, waiting for our blood, just for a little taste. Deep in the crevices as hate machinate, there lie the monsters of ancient times, rhymes at bedtime. Wake up, my children, blue marble, as we marvel, high in place as the sun does radiate.

All ill-fated monsters are true ventures to come, but they be not huge nor smelly with gnashing teeth, coming from some place deep, dark, hell-spawned beast...

Some may say these truths be good tidings, but what they are not abiding is that humankind brings such horrid tidings. The gaping hole, or whole, of inhumanity shall drive us all to the ends of sanity... lacking thy faith monsters lurk in such a place. Those true monsters are men no doubt I am now told.

Still, I hold, we shall be victorious in this battle of old... because from the darkest depths comes the light of thy heart whole... this love embrace "they" shall behold, never breaking God's Stronghold.

∞

| **Monsters in the Mirror** |

The enemy within, eroding, thwarting minds and hearts of men. Lacking courage to accept the truth of the enemy within, eroding, thwarting minds and hearts of men. Lacking courage to accept the truth of thy destruction is plain, preferring to cast blame, hiding within distorted ideologies postured over the slain.

Denying our collective garment, fiending turned cheeks steeped in inequities... inflicting sorrow over the plains blood stained. In lust hang "others" accursed in blame, in prose dreams of prosperity on the backs of thy brothers do you gain. Flailing capitalism born from Jim Crow laws. Reminiscent of restricted times, refusing to let blacks read the book of divine, back to banning books to keep children blind...racing toward fascist spells in *1984* did George Orwell tell.

Rejection of science, research, learning, anything generating critical thought, lap up tropes as fake news dopes, fear mongering a false form of hope. Claims for nostalgic past, swearing the children of slavery didn't suffer under thy lash. All to stop that inclusionist talk, full humanity squawk ... hardlines of superiority kind noose around my neck of inferiority times. Those who dare bespoke to be woke on diversity you choke.... You relish clout based on less than 1% genomic spout, you chose classism, and caste systems as the best route.

This MIND shall be our undoing. Acknowledge

thy histories, an infected misery upon the soul-journ of humanity, genetic fabric you refuse to see, past, present, future, will beseech thee. A fool reckoning, and fool's destiny.

What shall avail, open thy eyes, pull off the vail; justice is not a reward for sale. Lost soul wail, they quake in annihilation a living hell. Weeping inhumane, weeping pain, weeping so insane, gambling fiat for others to blame....as I lift my head, pressing down my pain, I shalt not bow again, as long as breathe, no matter how much I must bleed.

You shake your head, confused while sickened and amused.... You believe it's plain that I struggle in vain, that this is proof I must be insane.... But the size of a mustard seed I believe... I will bathe in the pain, washing away all stains, blame, and double-talk games. The courage I shall instill in my children is not in vain. With a prayer omittance of the stain of thy wicked reign...shall lay slain.

Monsters in the mirror... You know not my pain.

∞

| Ruler over We |

As we waiver in our circumference losing historical plight hopes take flight lifting the heavy yoke of tyranny from old, did we not strike...? An alleged independence fledging republic, on the lands of Indigenous tribal clans with new world plans.

Now in social space, decisions roll from a lofty place shrouding dreams of ego schemes... in alleyways we mock humanity's choreography. Our garments soaked in lime cannot dispel the stench of betrayal, with corrupted stories and tales.

Are we so coy it is future generations' we destroy—with twisted judiciary ploys—failing in our capacities and responsibilities...as we forsake. The unwise mental eyes, bequeathing presumptive immunity as alibis, supporting narratives of lies, reins of power as We the People die. It's not elusive that we the people are exclusive, hell bent on conclusive and preclusive... a selfish weighted backpack, funding super-pacs in support of diabolical pacts, while power brokers stalk foundational blocks, yearning for monarchs and oligarchs...

We reach peculiar shores with age-old lore designed in racial wars Plymouth bore a new land of capitalist prostitutes and whores... which has grown to mean production of more, extravagantly more as we implore. Covering voids we lust for, moral dilemmas selling our brethren when freedom is what they cry for. We rather harken to false lords, promises of wealth and riches by the sword. This is not a mythological tragedy... but now our modern-day realities.

We sacrifice humanity into caste to worship a trillionaire class. Such an odd pilgrimage this path we chose dominance a defunct path with ignorance sass of all past.

But alas Rise up my bludgeoned lass ...shake off trinkets for which we shrank, a lost sense of our divine rank and what is truly at stake.

The plea I bid thee, join in compassion of humanity, resist and do not flee, nor continue to forsake an inclusive We... If not for me, for our children we must plea, it is past time to cease thy racist ideology. Cannot we see none are truly free? Or must it be a broken land, foregone plan of liberty before you band as We.

This ravenous plate haste towards a dictator state... As we fornicate and intoxicate with racial hate, we are lost a soulless nation-state... a frozen mental state... beholden to those in High Towers lusting for Power, our Declaration they shall devour.

∞

∞ Shorts

| Walking through the Looking Glass |

We are multi-dimensional in our very essence, latching hold of who and what we think we are, coupled to the influential factors of the societal constructs. Amazingly, just as subatomic entanglement takes place, one being, one aspect of who we are, can be more than one facet and aspect of time and place. We tend to lean into the most upfront, crude course, but there is a dominant true self, stifled just below the surface of who we portray to the world. Our potential is vast, beyond the limitations of observable and measurable aspects of being. We are all things, everything, and nothing, all intertwined.

As we delve deeper into the looking glass of our hearts, souls, and minds, seizing the brightest beauty — not just of who we are, but stopping amidst the thick noise and vibrating chaos to realize the best of whom we can become. As we take stock, one aspect must be revealed: a parallel paradox unfolds in a completely different spatial dimension... walking all paths simultaneously without lapse or gaps, bound through an infinite universal thread... there is thy inverse, the greater verse of I, as one with the   Universe.

|| Tell the Truth and Shame the Devil ||

People enjoy telling others about their crap, shortcomings, failures, lack, and areas for additional expansion. On the other hand, we struggle to find the same degree of zeal to level up, work through our own crap, envy, jealousy, hate, distrust, greed, lust, unpack trauma, and continue learning to elevate our inner horizons by applying a growth mindset. Yes, absolutely tell the truth and shame the devil. That first starts within our hearts, minds, and spirits. All things are first connected within the self. If we aren't doing the work, who are we to persecute and judge others?

Be about the work so that we can transform the world and be the change we want to see.

|| My Mountain ||

Each morning, I wake and find myself at the base of Mount Kilimanjaro — a mountain I have never seen in this physical space. The mountain of the Children of the Moon. And each day, I attempt to traverse this mighty mountain.

Some days, I get very, very close to the crest, and I am excited, invigorated with the joy of potential and closeness of accomplishment. Other days, I barely make it one pace along the worn path I have made with this repeated journey. Then there are those days I dare not take a solitary step. I ball up as a child, fearful of the world and everything that lurks about.

I confess that some days are filled with hope, optimism, and thrill, while others seem broken, riddled with failure and inadequacies. Some days, as the sun begins to settle, I am filled with so much joy while other days some would say I am consumed with so much anguish and disappointment. I don't know exactly why each day can start and end so differently. Yet, each day, I find myself back at the base of Mount Kilimanjaro, deciding whether I even care to try.

On those days, I fear even taking one step. I search and search through my memories, heart, experiences, past and present, trying to determine if I am worthy of even being present before this mighty mountain. Why do I constantly return to this mountain day after day, striving and struggling to reach its heights, peak, pinnacle? What is it all for?

Then, as I sit contemplating the start of my day and how I have been here so many times before, a still voice whispers in my heart and spirit: "Just rise and take one step." I wrestle with that "why." I continue to hear this urging; sometimes it's in a voice familiar to me, a long-gone relative, a lost friend, a stranger, a foe, an unknown voice of antiquity. Yet, each day, I try to crest this mountain not knowing whether I will reach its top.

Oh Lord, on those days, I try! I try with the strength of generations, the hopes of nations, the love of the world, the passion of freedom, the struggle of justices, the commitment to right broken promises, the calling that we all are created equal, that we all are worthy, and the stirring of the soul that knows. One day!

One day soon! This mountain will be a minor hill in my journey put far behind me before I breathe my last breath.... Be it the will of the Most High and Beneficent Essence of All Life.

Amen.

|| Whirlwind within a Life ||

Not knowing you. Poem to a street hustler's child...

When I was first introduced unto you, had no idea nor clue what to do. Caught in a loveless life, street-hyped violence all too true, these things external well before you. It was all learned before having to consider a child like you.

Aim of game, street fame, vicious and insane, nothing could

change to include you. What in the world could I do? Because then along came you... pain wrestled through, now what one must do...? Torn between a life I deemed really true. Artificial space put between I and you... struggle with a world that didn't include you. How could I step when blood is how it is kept?

None understood claiming it a simple choice which seemed true, once being introduced to you. Mercilessly, I rode with my crew. This life was true, repping a heartless game to my sure undo.

Yet, how to continue now that there was someone as beautiful as you. The time and effort put in, to undo, people feared what I might do. Nightmares of what I could do, making violence so damn true. Still couldn't contemplate doing that unto you.

This is why it's true: I kept you a secret, too, so no one knew. Fear of what they may do, had they a clue. You were my only weakness in this world of what I knew. You couldn't understand how heartless I was in my head, chasing a game well before you were a thought, to the game I was true. But damn, after one look at you... What should I do? Fear of what might rain down upon you. The sins of a father must come due.

Courage I could not muster, contemplating untangling a web to somehow save you and still be true to a life set for my ruin and undo... contemplating a warrior's life to do better by you. Instead, I decided in my head to chase paper until dead for fear of loving you.

A life led guaranteed me dead, with wreckage and carnage .... all in my head, visions of me dead... as I lay on a street corner instead, bleeding out was my bed. Woke instead, raise from the undead... realizing I had a choice in my head.

Still with dread all in my head, how could I love you when I felt dead? But now I had to learn somehow to love you. My life in these streets I figured a warrior's path I could undo, but instead, I ended in four-by-fours with a bed, and a shank tucked in my bed... But damn certain, I was going to pull through, so I could get one more glimpse of you. Beautiful, so Beautiful, You.

|| Zebra ||

Child of adversity,

Child in a land of division.

I can't recall the first time I was called a "Zebra." It happened so often, other children casting it about playgrounds, hurling it across lunchrooms, hallways, and classrooms at school. It simply makes it difficult to remember the first time I'd been called it. At first, I really didn't understand the reference nor the meaning.

Then, as I started observing other families, I noticed that other children's parents seemed to be of the same hue or complexion as their children. I realized my parents were not the same hue nor complexion. In fact, my mother was very fair, while my father was a deep, rich, brown. This didn't trouble me; my parents separately expressed deep love towards me, inquiring about my well-being, asking how I was doing with schoolwork, what I had learned that day, what I enjoyed. Still, even with this sense of comfort, I wasn't ready to mention being called "Zebra" to my mother.

The question and reason behind "why" gnawed at me. Why weren't my parents the same hue or complexion as other parents? Aren't children supposed to be spitting images of one of their parents, if not both? I really wrestled with this question. I also started to note how adults would stare at me, flipping their eyes back and forth from my mother to me and back to her. In most cases, they would have this odd, snarling look on their faces while looking directly at me, cutting their eyes with a cold, hard look at my mother, a touch of disgust around their mouths. As if they could just spit upon us. But why? I couldn't comprehend what about us incited this response in people we didn't even know. They knew nothing about our family and didn't know anything about me.

At one point, in an attempt to rationalize this, I stumbled upon a thought: I must be adopted. This was the only logical explanation why adults and children couldn't make sense of my mismatched family. That had to be it. What else could explain such a broad public response everywhere and anywhere we went? The only problem was, this went against what my mother had told me since I was a baby... that "You are my baby, and I love you so."

Why couldn't the world around me see that love and accept us for just being us?

Controversy can break cultures, and difference within a social construct steeped in racist theology eats away at the collective strength of all communities.

|| Your Hate Has No Place ||

No halva nor hole to hide.

Hate is powerless unless we give it space and place to grow. Hate drains time, energy, and life force, requiring intentional effort to be hosted.

Hate is insecure; it must control to conceal the mask of fears and inadequacies imposed through violence upon others.

Hate is ignorance. Hate is oppressive to independence of will, seeking to poison that which harbors its.

Hate limits, demanding conformity narrowing our scope and span, strangling potential, caught in a blind inability to connect with our collective humanity.

Hate debilitates hearts and minds, fueling delusions of

grandeur in misguided thoughts of dominance, superiority, power.

Hate resides in lower-level thinking, undercutting the authentic ability of human beings... entertaining animalistic views, desires, thoughts, concepts.

Hate cuts off our genuine power, grace, and majesty to manifest our unlimited potential as a human family connected to the essence of all life.

Hate is a death sentence gripping people in stagnation, a selfish child birthed alternatively to the embrace of the Supreme Essence, an inability to confidently stand before the beauty and life-giving light of truth.

Thus, we as warriors have made it our pastime to snatch the devil out of the frame. We are coming... kicking in doors on chambers of deception; there is no place, no halva nor hole to hide with thy lies.

Hate despises the light of truth because we come with proof, show and prove unto the youth. We will see thee in the light, through our plight, which is light work to that of inspiration though you wish it to burden us hoping we would break.

|| Damn, It Is Insane ||

We are approaching this all wrong. Racism is a form and condition of insanity — but not in any studied mental health way. Believing a person or group of people is exalted and superior above all other human beings is a delusion of superegos stoking self-appointed grandeur. It's a mindset that takes historical events, such as the systematic slaughter of Indigenous and Native people for land and calls it "manifest destiny." It justifies land-grab expansions, systematic reappropriation of lands while painting a narrative that the people who once resided there were savage and undeveloped when the real savagery was committed against the Indigenous and Native people.

Racism enslaves an entire group of people based upon race, stripping them of identity, culture, language, dignity, and humanity and reducing them to the level of beasts based upon a false narrative of inferiority then coupling it to "Black Codes" twisted as perverse benevolence, while portraying brutality, murder, rape, forced labor, an economic stranglehold, and oppression of "Blacks" as upliftment. Systemic cruelty and hateful ignorance perpetuated over some 400-odd years.

And even now, depicting the legal rolling back of civil rights, mechanisms of inclusion, women's rights, and human rights due to systemic ignorance, and pitching Diversity Equity & Inclusion (DEI) practices as somehow standing for reverse racism and disenfranchisement of the dominant culture and class...is hypocrisy at its finest. Of course, it doesn't stop there. The persecution of people for experiencing and loving differently than a dominant culture of straight, heterosexual male stances of relationships — cloaked in pseudoscience to support proposed "reeducation and therapy" — exposes the extent of delirium. Treachery runs deep in the hearts of those who desire absolute control.

Look through historical events, eras, epochs, regimes, colonization, exploitation, suppression, genocides, claims of racial supremacy, economic pillaging, the bloody extraction of labor, the Trail of Tears while tearing people from their homelands, and the vicious advocacy of caste systems for societal control...the results and outcomes are all the same: destruction of human potential. The propagation of false storylines put forth to the world over and over again of entitlement, of self-anointed rulership, the constant vicious calculation and lust for maintenance of systems to control and hold power to lord over the rest of humanity based on a twisted belief of being superior compared to all other humans. And yet that's not the kicker...

It is the repetition of these beliefs and actions, an adulterated denial of humanity of all other human beings...with a demand, we acquiesce to a mental model that places one race above all others with shades of gray in DNA... wrapped in a culture, processes, procedures, of existential reinforcement to hold a brutal reign. To think repeating this carnage will change the outcomes and subdue the truth of humanity's spirit while expecting everyone everywhere to believe in this nightmare for centuries, repeating the deceptions again and again, while passing off these transgressions and offenses ...as divine providence... Is insane!

And stoking it as some form of anointed destiny, washing over all imagery and saviors as white to instill mental concepts of racial hierarchy. To further solidify, dare we say, a proclamation as lord over Humanity. When in fact, this mindset is so far from anything divine, with roots, steeped in racist regurgitated bile, to hide the hand dragging our world towards pure chaos. We must declare this diabolical violence as confirmation of one diagnosis: racism, in all its forms, is Insanity. Racism, generation after generation, continues with its paper tiger symptoms of superiority, is a racist's inability to face the reality of its heinous impact on humanity.

So, we shall not be enablers of hate, violence, ignorance, and the falsity that allows bigotry to continue stealing the beauty and joy from the rest of humanity! Nor shall we continue to enable tactics expanding mental oppression and suppression, driven by psychosis.

> *"Insanity is doing the same thing over and over again but expecting different results."*
>
> **—Rita Mae Brown**
> **(1983 novel *Sudden Death*)**

We refuse your tired line that "change takes time"... Spare us, this isn't our first rodeo, son... We know what bull crap smells like... History tells us so. And so do all the barriers, obstacles, closed doors, broken roads/promises, disenfranchisement, threats, acts of violence, and murders to deter our hearts... We aren't going for that either. We sing, marched, dreamed beautiful dreams, and plead again and again with your tyrannical-minded ass. We finally know your condition. Sadly, we cannot help you until you take the first step toward recovery: acknowledging that "You are the root cause".

Meanwhile, the soul of a loving people is mighty. We can no longer avoid the truth, for corruption spreads, lurking in the heart, casting distrust, division, and hate continuing the destruction of us all. So, yes, we shall move forward! Yes, we shall open doors, build on-ramps to equity, foster inclusive relationships, and establish missions of diversity, nurturing authentic belonging. We shall join together under the banner of collective good, refusing to give up our seats or step aside, while dismantling the matrix of coded hate. We are not going around back, nor bowing our heads, begging for acceptance nor defined token positions in a racist hierarchy. We shall not be your booger boo. Mighty is the spirit of humanity, and the truth does indeed liberate us all!

So, until you step forward and acknowledge the insanity of what you have done and continue to do — the festering poison in the echo chamber of your mind — we'll be busy building our neighbors up and forging communities with people who have had enough of your blood-soaked path. It's time to love those who yearn for true love and want to thrive in community. Until then, we will relentlessly expose who you are: the seed of Insane Hate. Unless, of course, you are hell bent on demonstrating the folly in our faith that knowledge is the remedy for ignorance, wisdom the embodiment of our actions, understanding an exalted form of love, all culminating in the redemption of humanity. Then my Friend, the next time is the Fire!

|| Why Share Our Thoughts & Experiences ||

Exchange to stimulate.

Sharing our thoughts and experiences as they relate to our lives immersed in an experiment of being. Our broader human network of being — interactive through social justice, equitable practices, and diverse perspectives — lays a foundation for inclusion that nurtures sincere belonging.

It's not about convincing every person that it's a worthy cause or that we need a restrictive framework of conformity on how to do better. It's more about sharing our insights to learn from one another and knowing we aren't alone in this journey, as well as a belief that more humans than not want to do good rather than exploit and monetize every aspect of life. That's important to reinforce, decoupling from a user to a giver and contributor to humanity.

Our life experiences are not geared in sharing eloquent perfectionism through a false medium to accumulate things, nor is it necessarily leaning into heavy hard knowledge transfers. We seek to amplify transparency, and authenticity, to grow through a lens of vulnerability, sharing energy with one another, to motivate, inspire, and hopefully liberate ourselves from mental shackles of imposed categorization. Releasing the millstone of hate from upon our souls and stepping into our Power, as Warriors for true Love.

|| When We Move In ||

Proximity.

"Love thy neighbor as thy love thy self."

We seem to continuously refer to love or getting along. Yet, how does this mesh with our ability to accept, embrace, be kind, thoughtful, and helpful toward those who don't think, act, or come from the same socio-economic class, cultures, or home/family dynamics as us? Or those who simply don't look like us?

Do we claim to be good people from a distance if "they" remain at arm's length? Are we good people in words and deeds? Are we capable of demonstrating authentic humanity towards "all" human beings? Are we doing more than outward window dressing to receive accolades as a "Good Person"? Are we sincerely demonstrating "compassion" toward others?

Each individual must answer these questions sincerely within their hearts. Heed the light that shines through layers of excuses cloaking over spoken intentions that are not actuated. We all have the ability to do better and grow.

It takes work and doesn't happen when we are trying to extinguish authentic discussions, eliminate diverse narratives, or sterilize learning through a dominant culture of betrayal. Social good, social justice, social equality, social inclusion, social belonging, social access to resources, and representation are more than singular perspectives; they aren't confined to one group, one way, one class, one people.

Nor is it one message, mission, or group above another nor others. And it isn't just one organization. It is a multifaceted message, mission, and groups of people coming together to make our world a better place for all. Time to get comfortable with being uncomfortable. It's past time to be the positive change we desire in this world.

|| What You Can't Stop ||

You may believe you've stopped or blocked us based upon perceived power, control, or influence. Truth is, it's really a temporary pause, a minor hurdle, a detour, if you will, to a bigger purpose and meaning to it all.

What you can't stop are ideas, thoughts, insights, questioning inner spirits and the imagination of what can be. That's well beyond your childish mechanisms of control or temporal power.

So, you do you, Boo-Boo, because we for damn certain are going to do and be us. You're not the all-seeing, all-knowing as you deluded yourself to believe. Even with all the cyber surveillance and tech you can muster.

We gotcha... it's that time!

|| I Am a Good Person ||

What does working to become our best selves mean to you?

How long of a journey is that? Does it ever truly end?

How will I know that I am growing, showing, and proving?

Who should accompany me on this learning journey?

How will I know that I am engaging with the right people along the way?

What resources are necessary to grow and become my best self?

Can I recall a time where I felt deeply and authentically included? Has this experience taken place at a social gathering, within an employee resource group, in an educational environment, or while researching a subject of particular interest?

What exact elements nurture or stimulate inclusive and/or equitable connectivity with others?

"Equity refers to being provided with equal opportunity in all segments of society, including support, fairness, and equitable outcomes[2]."

"Inclusion is the practice of including all, providing opportunities for those who otherwise would be marginalized[3]."

What are you sincerely doing as a leader to facilitate an equitable and inclusive space for people to thrive?

These are questions we really must grapple with to develop executable plans for realization. Our current social construct is about grinding against human potential. Imagine a pivotal shift, to one of investing, cultivating, and nurturing human potential.

Imagine the strength and beauty we could birth into the world!

|| We Must Have Courage ||

"One isn't necessarily born with courage,
but one is born with potential.
Without courage, we cannot practice any
other virtue with consistency.
We can't be kind, true, merciful,
generous, or honest."

— **Maya Angelou (1988)**

To be human is to know our capacity, to bear witness to the range of compassion and cruelty.

Double-speak and forked tongues usurp acknowledgment of thy inner power. Terms and conditions as they arbitrarily define. Strong but not too strong. Independence in thoughts but not beyond being reigned in. Voice but not without a muzzle. Vision but not without bowing to defined parameters.

Courage yet not without fear of the controlling establishment. Change without disruption. Freedom but with

---

[2] Questions in Qualitative Social Justice Research in Multicultural Contexts by Anna CohenMiller, Nettie Boivin.
[3] CohenMiller & Boivin.

shackles. Be true to you without speaking thy truth.

Love within defined frameworks of love. Freedom but on terms. Ideas but based on predisposed context. Bold while reminded to cower down, know thy place. Spirit but not ferocious. Rules of systems of suppression and control subtly expressed.

Innovation only within prescribed boxes to drive commerce. Creativity without originality. Speak candidly without candor, without exposing shortfalls. Growth without challenging others to grow. Peace without the struggle of war or discomfort.

Humanity but only as defined. Human rights without hindering financial sourcing. Liberty without justice. Freedom without being free.

Spirituality with blinders as a traditional control mechanism. Freedom of speech while being suitable to the establishment.

Uphold ideals through sanctioned applications that don't stimulate true education. Dissent without disagreement.

All based upon narrow minds... to produce more narrow minds. Docile are the times.

‖ Vote ‖

The easiest thing is to complain yet do nothing to influence different outcomes. Thus, we can't claim to want change if we don't participate or engage.

A strategy of oppression against social justice, equity, diversity, and inclusion mindset is disenfranchisement. The worst part is that many of us are stuck in generational cycles that make us feel powerless, leading us to give up. We claim nothing will change; "they" are just going to do what "they" want. The notorious "they" are nefariously behind every scene of failed change.

The worst part is that this mysterious phantom "they" has trained us to acquiesce through our own inaction. We give up, don't try, and refuse to participate because "they" hold all the power. Yet, we fail to recognize that we give them power over us through inaction, non-participation, and refusing to do anything different. We hand over control of our nation's course, policies, agendas, and strategies.

Their best tactic is to stick people into a frozen state of existence, birthing generation upon generation of mental servitude. By mentally beating people down, they discourage us from even trying. Then "they" can shape and fashion things however "they" want, while we, as opponents, don't even show up on the battlefield. That's unacceptable.

It's time we push back on these concepts and refuse to accept "they" as omniscient in power. The truth is, they are not. It's not that we must be brave, strong, smart, charismatic, possess extreme wealth, be reckless, or hyper militant. We already have a right to participate — that's one of our mechanisms to push back.

And we must push back because others sacrificed, fought hard, survived, escaped, ran, helped others, hid, risked their lives, dared not give up a seat, defiantly marched, peacefully resisted, withstood abuse, cared, dreamed, hoped, and loved for us to one day have this right. We have had it for a while now. Not to mention people from all walks of life have fought in every battle, war, major campaign, and revolution in this country. So, we shouldn't take this responsibility lightly since people gave their blood to certify our right to cast a ballot.

Please don't give this right back simply because "they" don't want us to be counted. Whoever "they" are. Don't let them take something so precious away from us without giving the good fight. We cannot say "they" have absolute control if we give up and give it to them through our own inaction. We mock the sacrifices of so many with our inaction.

Don't give up without putting forth stiff resistance — if it is all a lie, then let's make sure "they" know we aren't going to just lie down. Let's make sure "they" know intimidation tactics aren't enough, lies aren't enough, their trillionaire friends aren't enough, their super-pacs aren't enough, their hateful taunts aren't enough, their redistricting and redlining aren't enough. Let's make sure our voices are heard through our vote, and resistance. Let's learn about core issues and concerns, not accepting rhetoric on face value. And organize in a manner that we can support candidates based on substantive actions in support of our priorities. If there isn't a candidate aligned with our positions, then we need to petition to get those issues center stage — or run ourselves.

And if "they" want to truly suppress democracy, utterly failing those ideals of freedom, justice, equality, liberty, and the right to pursue happiness because "they" want a caste system, an ignorant system, a bigoted system, an oppressive system, a racist system, a system of ruling classes... Let's make sure "they" know it is at their own peril.

Vote early, vote local, vote state, vote federal, vote nationally — by all means, vote.

"Let me point out to you that freedom is not something that anybody can be given; freedom is something people take and people are as free as they want to be. One hasn't got to have an enormous military machine in order to be un-free when it's simpler to be asleep, when it's simpler to be apathetic, when it's simpler, in fact, not to want to be free, to think that something else is more important".

— **James Baldwin, Nobody Knows My Name (July 1961).**

|| Usual Suspects ||

Who are your usual suspects?

Bias, stereotypes, bigotry, ignorance, hate, receiver, taker, user, oppressor, entitlement, self-righteousness, discrimination, favoritism, privilege, classism, thinking something is owed to you?

Or thoughtfulness, humanity, collaboration, giver, kindness, inclusion, learning, teacher, encouragement, constructive criticism, empower, sharer of insights (wisdom), supportiveness, leaning into understanding, identifying common ground, belonging, emotional intelligence?

We have choices in the difference and impact we can make in this life, and that is largely based upon our approach and mentalities.

Choose wisely, my friends.

|| Upon This Hill We Shall Give Our All ||

We can do better, we have done better at various times, and we are better when we set our hearts and minds to Be Better. We are no longer sold on doing what we are told... the Battleground of Differences is being used to hyper-polarize to assault our humanity. We continue to let so-called leaders weaponize the beauty of difference to pit people, pitting US, against one another. To what avail? Who really gains as we channel our potential and resources against one another?

We allow narrow self-serving egos and arrogance to convulse against the truth of life. They cannot and will not accept that life does not center around them... so-called dominant culture isn't the qualifier of all that is true, good, strong, beautiful, or brilliant. Unfortunately, we have a preponderance of leaders that would rather toe some arbitrary lines beholden to power dynamics. This strategy, mindset, and stance all come at the expense of the people they should be advocating for and championing.

It is time we, the People, people who are actively working for an inclusive world, acknowledge this sad truth and start advocating and championing for ourselves... not based on hidden agendas, backroom deals, winks, handshakes, head nods, extortion, or financial payoffs of support or promises of appointment to coveted positions. We are the catalyst for freedom, justice, equality, equity, inclusion, access, and humanity.

We are the "only" ones who can make that true for all. To hell with these puppets who fear the established system of things, who sell us on paths of patience, perseverance, struggle, suffering, and hardship in the name of so-called savvy gamesmanship. We end up bearing the burden while they sit as lapdogs groveling at the feet of trillionaires and power brokers for backing and support.

They have ignored our pleas, our appeals to humanity, our call for caring, kindness, protection, and love for ALL PEOPLE. We can no longer sit back as our voices go unheard and unheeded. We must break our silence and compliance, taking a stance for life, liberty, rights to exist, and pursue thriving and vibrant happiness. We must break the yoke and mental shackles of servitude. While these so-called leaders continue to rationalize that We the People don't understand how things "really" work! That change takes centuries, and that is the damn problem....

Our leaders adopt mentalities geared in support of suppressive systems, policies, behaviors, and ways of doing that buttress dominant cultures' agendas and endgame to our demise. They have us captively frozen, with a stranglehold upon the necks of our freedom. This is why they want us to pipe down, give it time, let the process work, let diplomacy resolve things.... And this mindset and mentality "allows" the continued heaping of injustice, atrocities, genocide, and hypocrisy to proliferate and expand exponentially.

What we are witnessing isn't leadership. This isn't strength. This isn't in the best interest of humanity... It is all self-serving motives, Machiavellianism, and a play to hold positions of power instead of taking a position of POWER for truth and humanity. No more, no damn more! The burden of injustice is just too high a price to pay, while losing our hearts and souls in the process of occupation, mental colonization, murdering the spirit of freedom!

We must accept the truth. Our future, our humanity, our rights to self-determination are not a game. It is truly a matter of life and death, as well as the future for generations to come.... It sincerely is an inflection point of life versus death — oppression — suppression — mental bondage by the hand of those who have become beholden to an extreme degree of ignorance, a racist caste system in the high castle, and a way of life resting a boot upon our necks... all human beings. We must say no more, take a stance of no more, and start to lead from within moored upon a rock of love and truth within our hearts, leading with compassion and humanity from within.

Upon this hill we shall make our stand!

|| Understanding Our Part ||

Limitations of self-hate.

We rage against the exploitive machine of things, with its systemic suppression of diverse thought, oppression of authentic humanity, lies of exalted racial categories, and corruption of our connectivity as people. Yet, we have to really look within. How much of that do we propagate, directly and inadvertently, through our own actions and deeds? Are we contributing to disparities with our complacency, our complicit and implicit biases?

We must eliminate our own self-hate as well as hatred of others. We cannot effect substantive change without first becoming anew in our mentalities and shifting our ring-leader roles within a dysfunctional societal dynamic.

It all starts within the self. We can claim to be "good people," espousing so-called strong "moral values." Yet, if we are not actively applying, living, growing, and championing these in how we engage others, neighbors, community members, society, and the world at large, it's all for naught.

Have a great day, my friends. And take care.

|| Today is Always the Day ||

Today is the battleground for future generations.

Tomorrow is not promised, while today is always the day we have to act. To raise our voices, take initiative, institute change, counter lies, disrupt false narratives, dislodge microaggressions, trip up hate, stop violence, expose bigotry, extend a helping hand, offer words and deeds of encouragement, demonstrate kindness, be allies, make a difference, fight the good fight, start the journey, express authentic love for all people, stand up for truth, implement equitable access to programs, advocate for justice, become champions for freedom, break the silence on harmful tactics, call people out on their ignorance, pull the blindfold off of liberty, shine a light upon hypocrisy. Today, today, today. Not tomorrow, nor the next day.

Why are you waiting for tomorrow, my friends? Tomorrow is not promised, but what is certain is that we have today!

|| Ego Distorts the Ability to See Others ||

Don't expect egotistical, entitled, privileged people to recognize our potential. At worst, they will want us to toil under them, and at best, they will use us in the pursuit of exploitative agendas. We must first recognize our own worth, forgive our trespasses, and ignite the glow of love within our own hearts. Then embrace it, allowing the light from within to manifest through our thoughts, ideas, actions, and behaviors, demonstrating to the world what the narrow-minded are unable to perceive as a superpower.

Being humble isn't weak, demonstrating consideration and kindness towards others isn't being soft, and lending a helping hand is not being taken advantage of. Humanity is real. We have lost our way with these self-centered haughty false prophets of change. They are charlatans playing the role of courageous Lions, yet just beneath the surface they are shallow superficial petty thieves groveling about as jackals nipping at the heels of those striving to be upright.

Dare to be bold. Dare to be courageous. Dare to be free!

|| Take Straight Bets with Inevitable Odds ||

We must strive each and every day to raise the bar of Humanity. Even when things seem bleak, we must step up to bring the heat and compete. We don't shake off microaggressions, violence, the distortions of facts, and attempts to perpetuate systemic oppression... as some form of blessing, pawned off as acceptable bigotry. The premise we are expected to just roll with it. Try as you might to sanitize the pillaging and usurping of cultures, but that only works on those who are mentally submissive and paralyzed by fear. You delude yourselves, embracing spells of complicit silence, inaction, and complacency.

Don't forget, the light of truth exposes that which comes from darkest of hearts. The fact that ignorance, hate, and violence are openly on display and celebrated shows the pressure of change is coming. Racist wrap themselves in the garment of reversed racism, with false claims of rooting out discriminatory practices while holding privilege and established seats of power, laying bare how much they revile mechanisms of authentic inclusion for all people.

Freedom, justice, equality, liberty, equity, shared power, and the pursuit of happiness are great ideals... until that includes all human beings, requires sharing power, requires equitable access to resources, requires equitable outcomes, isn't just for them, frees the yoke of servitude, liberates all classes of people, dispels preferential treatment, disrupts caste systems, upsets disparities, disrupts practices/procedures/behaviors that sanction "white" as right. Topples the lie of a racial pyramid that seats select people as rulers over all people.

See, that is how we expose the racists. They'd much rather destroy concepts advocating for real democracy than embrace all humanity in an inclusive manner. They will pursue feudalism, lords, ruling classes, ruling families, oligarchies, and monarchies... They will destroy all things before they include, empower, and truly love.

That is how this twisted little tale of betrayal comes full circle with the founding of a nation, by the colonies... wrought in contradiction and peculiar institutions... because they know deep down it was initiated in gamesmanship... especially if the result means sharing with all people. We are witnessing the reaping of the bigger deception that was told, bought and sold through the American Dream.

See, we truly believe in that Dream, as I have a Dream, absent the nightmares. We champion these great ideals... rolling down a mighty mountain, founded upon the evident truth in our hearts that all people are created equal. Now, we will show and prove whether this Dream is one of compassion and love or if it is the contradiction of those who now realize it must extend to all... or demonstrate the falsity of it all. Letting the world know the emperor has no clothes.

|| Speak Your Truth ||

Sharing positive energy empowers.

Sharing our experiences, situations endured, and jewels of insight is powerful. It's an exchange and flow of energy, growth, knowledge, wisdom, and understanding that allows us to elevate to that next level in degrees of learning.

Not everyone gets that. Not everyone understands the thread of humanity in sharing our narratives, nor can they comprehend the significance of leaning into our collective connection. Why is that?

Too many folks are incorrigible caught up in a sterile culture of control, boxed in by restrictive thinking and narrow perspectives of being. They're acting like robots coded into thinking within specific confines; if it doesn't fit the framework as told, they revert to attempting to control others through conformance because that's all they know, as prescribed and sanctioned by colonizer thinking.

It reminds me of a saying we used on the railroad: "Railroading is for everybody, but not everyone is for railroading." There's a lot of wisdom in that saying, reaching well beyond railroading. A slight twist on it: "Truth is for everyone, but not everyone is for truth." That's real in so many ways.

Tabitha Brown, in her book *Feeding the Soul (Because It's My Business): Finding Our Way to Joy, Love, and Freedom*, spoke about something very similar when expressing how truth spoken in the heart and spirit is an especially prescribed medicine to heal our souls.

The medicine for healing you isn't necessarily for everyone else. My prescription for healing may not be for you. And that's okay. My purpose is about helping those I can. Helping those who need to hear a message tailored for them because they have endured, soul-journed, are currently experiencing or confronted with situations/circumstances very similar to those I express and share. This medicine, this truth, this insight, this understanding, is for everyone, but not everyone is ready or able to accept that healing. That's all right; they'll get the appropriate medicine, hopefully in due time, and probably from another source that rings true for them.

Disease or dis-ease comes in many forms, but not everyone recognizes something is wrong. I learned that during my residencies for my Ph.D. research. There are three groups in research: those that recognize anomalies in the data research process and develop a method to account for it, completing the analysis with clear explanations; then there's the group that recognizes the anomalies in the data, acknowledges it as a limitation, but are not certain of the proper methodology to address it; finally, there are those who are completely oblivious to the anomalies within the data research process and proceed without awareness nor recognize how it impacts the outcomes of what they are studying, nor their claimed findings.

The same is very true in this life. Some of us will recognize things aren't right and will work to correct those injustices and inequities. Others amongst us will see things that are wrong, speak to it, but are unclear on just how to resolve it. And finally, there will be those completely unaware, just droning along, not even understanding nor attempting to fulfill their potential. Such is life. Yet, it doesn't have to be that way.

In short, my friends, we must stay on mission, advocate our truth, be strong, share vulnerability, and manifest our light from within as radiant beacons of guidance for those who know something is wrong but are not quite certain how to correct it. Just understand there will be some amongst us who will choose to remain oblivious, who are not only unaware but refuse to raise their heads from the trough of miseducation, indoctrination, closed minds, closed hearts, with stiff necks, and rebelliousness to a world that is inclusive of all humanity. This too shall only last for a season.

|| Sower of Seeds ||

Sower of seeds, casting ideas. The distinction of the seed is whether it will germinate, which depends largely upon the soil of the mind. Soil of the mind can be deep and rich for ideas to flourish and grow, or barren wastelands of ignorance, hard and dry land unable to expand beyond what it is told. Not every mind shall be fertile with the "will" to produce fruits of independence and critical thinking.

This leads to a thought in historical times, an idea leaped forward from a small group of colonies wrapped in many contradictions and strange institutions. Still, these colonies embraced a radical concept to take a stance against tyranny. An even smaller group of people within those colonies latched on to an idea of revolution against leadership that suppressed human rights. They dared to demand the ability to pursue things such as self-determination, representation of the people, independence, freedom of determination, and justice taxation. Odd how these concepts sprang from colonies that failed to extend those principles beyond a select group... some say it was the limitations of the times.

But now, we stand in a time when people have once again latched on to "ideas," to have the ability to seek — no, dare we say pursue — self-determination, representation of the people, independence, freedom, justice, and equality. These claims seem so foreign to many citizens who have been denied "full access," relegated to second-class citizenry, if you will. We struggle for freedom of thought, breaking away from the dominant culture that demands we fit into sterile definitions of who and what we should or can be.

Are we revolutionary when we say freedom of thought and nonconformity is an aspect of our independence? We run the risk of losing life, bodily harm, or the ability to pursue a livelihood for not harboring a conformist mind, a docile, laden mind. Such a contradictory story, to build a nation upon principles of freedom, justice and liberty, yet deny these same principles to other humans. Is there really any wonder as to why we see the pendulum swinging to extremists trying to wrestle for control of all branches of government?

To challenge authority or group thinking has become an alien concept. To expect "public servants" or leading from a stance of noble purpose, to serve the public and humanity for the greater good is now an oddity. Even more odd, raising a voice for humanity is not permissible, chic, or condoned unless sanctioned by big money groups, special interests, approved dominant culture, and tyrant certified. These all have been twisted into running the risk of being labeled unpatriotic or anti-this or that. Just for taking a stance for freedom from "neo-tyranny".

At this point, we mark the full circle of the life cycle of an once underdog fledgling nation, now headlong plunging toward fascism and demagoguery, pressing throughout the world scene as the new villain.

The Revolutionary Samuel Adams says Samuel Adams worried about, *"To have a villainous ruler imposed on you was a misfortune. To elect him yourself was a disgrace."*

Ironically, here we are, little colonies all grown up... toying with the ideas of ruling classes, oligarchies, monarchies, and fascism, with the face mask of trillionaires and elitism.

Strange, even while witnessing this perilous plunge, I propose we are still worth fighting for, and there is still time to save the soul of our nation, maybe even the world if we, all the people, have the will and faith to fight and sacrifice for what is right... authentic humanity, sincere freedom, justice, and equality, with liberty for all. And this round we do mean, All the people.

|| Societal Extermination ||

What happens when people perceive a societal construct as designed to negate the fundamental essence of who they are?

One, it creates an existence of friction. As time continues, societal negation will grind away all things and all those who don't align to its design. Thus, a dynamic tipping point springs forth. You push back and you disrupt with every fiber of your being in opposition to becoming a conformist. Because to not do so means to algin with a plan set for your annihilation.

|| Social Cyclops ||

Blue light blind

With ease, we hate from afar, basking in catchphrases, trite clap backs, and swirls of misinformation bashing against other humans, undermining our humanity. The explosion of our connectivity is both a gift and a cautionary tool.

I recall when I first learned how to use a pocketknife as a tool—cutting rope, carving sticks, throwing at boards—as a weapon of defense, and, eventually, the harm one could inflict. But multiple diligent instructors were also there to guide me at a young age, providing context, methods, and implied outcomes. Respecting tools and weapons, their versatility and usefulness, guided by purposeful thought, recognizing their potential for good while alternatively understanding that we wield the power to commit harm.

Unfortunately, there are no firm instructional guides accompanying social media as a tool. Yes, each platform presents terms of use, how-tos, and easy reference shortcuts, yet within, there are no instructions on how the tool can be used to spread truth alongside falsehood, enlighten or deceive hearts, invoke good or disseminate elements of destruction... None are given real tutelage on responsibility, guided intentions, or defining the range of impact, to influence, persuade, conflict, cast doubt, or ignite contention... tools are defined by the mentalities of those who pick them up to cast about or emit doubt.

We'd rather sit next to one another on a train or plane, stand together in line... barely an arm's reach away... living reality side by side as humans; yet our worlds are catapulted apart while we scroll, click, swipe, and smite... ignoring one another's presence, reading the scribblings and doodles of influencers we haven't had the pleasure of accompanying in the same space. Hell, all we know, they could be light years away for how far apart we have become while standing nearby.

We've made ourselves somehow captivated and disconnected in our quest for connectivity. Captive to a social cyclops vomiting AI driven algorithms of rabbit hole connectivity, while secretly eroding our collective humanity. We fear experiencing one another in the real... concerned that we will be had, took, bamboozled, tricked, embarrassed, played a fool or ridiculed... In turn, we prefer to cast our lot with those far and wide for their wit, smiles of screen beauty, enticing, smooth soothsayers, and filters of beauty yet truly unknown.

Look up, my friends. See the people to your right, to your left, or even behind you, experiencing the world just as you are, in that place, in that moment of real. Maybe we can pull our tilted heads away momentarily from the social cyclops we hold to see one another through a lens of human experience...be present in thy circumferences of exchange, sharpen, challenge, provoke, learn, grow, maybe even listen to another nearby. Don't be mastered by the tools you were meant to wield...that now seem to wield power over us... connecting to other humans is how we nurture our inner humanity... and is the source code to the essence of all life.

Step into the cipher, my friends. Know who holds the power to power down, my friends.

|| See You on the Flip Side, Know-It-All ||

For the pompous mind: If you know everything, why are you here amongst those of us who don't know anything? Especially if you aren't teaching or sharing your expansive wealth of knowledge. It seems pointless for you to be here, doesn't it?

Life is about learning, experiences, communicating, connecting, and identifying one's innermost potential and purpose... Of course, you already understand and know all that. So, the bigger question remains: why are you even here amongst us mere mortals?

Ah, that's right—so you can walk around acting entitled, self-assured, as if the rest of the world owes you something.

Guess what? See you on the flip side, know-it-all.

|| Power to Save Ourselves ||

Stop waiting upon another!

Check out this article by Roxane Gay: "Remember, No One Is coming to Save Us[4]."

People can inspire, motivate, and encourage us to elevate above mediocre standards of existence. Still, they can only ignite a spark of light and directionality that resides within us if we are working to thrive and flourish. We must understand our paragons are ever-growing, expanding in thoughts, ideals, understandings, and actions to nurture positive impacts in our communities, broader society, and world.

It would be great if everything in the world would come together seamlessly. Yet, change—leveling of basic human interactions whereby people treat other humans equitably with

---

[4] https://www.nytimes.com/2020/05/30/opinion/sunday/trump-george-floyd-coronavirus.html

kindness—requires work. Authentic caring is a crucible element, we do not simply walk into it. We must be tenacious in living it.

To do so, we must reckon with our social construct, which is wired towards a hyper self-centered super-ego that makes it arduous for people to veritably embrace intersectionality as foundational to our larger human connection. The failed trade-off is worship of a golden calf (material possessions and monetization of everything), adoration of our lives calculated through a lens of "what's in it for me."

We've decoupled ourselves from our oneness with the commonality of humanity. We dribble about 1 or 2 percent of racial difference, ignoring 98 to 99 percent of inherent togetherness. Thus, we squander our human potential while allocating large sums of energy and potential fighting to maintain racial segmentation and classism of populations to claim exalted status based in no scientific significance. It boils down to petty disputes of power, control, and subjugation.

We must re-learn, or start to learn in some cases, how to sincerely love ourselves as a human family, moving beyond narrow worship of arbitrary racial qualifiers over all others. Suppression of our inner light that emits from within crushes the capacity to elevate as a species. The sad part is, we unwittingly waste the power of *will* in our choices to lord over human beings.

Our choices are decisive inflection points. What do you choose?

|| Radical Workouts ||

Change is like a workout: it all starts with the first rep. Initially, your very first push-up will be uneven. You'll probably only be able to do a partial pull-up, perform wobbly curls, have an awkward stride while jogging, or strain to do a handful of crunches. Everything will seem difficult and painful. In the very beginning, form will not be the focus; it will not matter so much.

What does matter is that you've shown up, you have started the process, and you are finally "doing something" to move the needle in a better direction.

Change, honestly, is that work, and it is no different, folks. During your first workout, pretty much everything will seem new, different, and uncomfortable. But you're there, and you're in the process. And it is meant to be ongoing. Whether you just want to improve your mental health, improve your fitness as a human being, endurance to engage tough questions, strength during trying times, or move beyond appearance and build longevity, recover from years of inactivity during which the community has struggled, or simply want to transform the world around you, it all starts uncomfortably.

Change is onerous at times. Working out can be uncomfortable as hell, especially the next day if you were really focused, putting in work, and striving to reach your personal best at that time. That is important... your personal best will not look like everyone else's, and it will evolve over time.

What is important is that you stay committed, you keep showing up, and you keep putting in work. Now, some days, you will feel like a freaking rockstar. You'll feel like you are starting to get the hang of it, and there will be a sense of accomplishment. On other days, your efforts will not seem good enough. What you do give will fall short, and others will side-eye you. That happens.

Every day is different. Some will seem mundane, lackluster, and we walk away feeling like crap. It's life, it's real, and nothing is supposed to be easy about it. On the flip side, there will be days you are putting in some serious work, knocking down reps like a champ and you will feel like you are victorious... then you will run into someone who will blow you literally out of the water. They will lap you; they will out-press you; they will do twice what you can do at your personal best, all while making the work look very damn easy. Guess what? That is all right too. You must push and pace yourself... because you don't want to injure yourself, crash out, burn out, or fall out completely. We all have a personal best, a stride... it is about "our" progress. It's about that consistency.

Still, that doesn't mean half-stepping or not making any progress at all. You must continue to raise the bar, add additional reps, push another half-mile, stack another wheel on, add more sets, and incorporate different muscle areas, and types of workouts to continue along this journey. It doesn't stop until we draw our last breath. A warrior for substan

tive change shall not be satisfied!

Change doesn't stop simply because a specific group of people "feel" we have done enough. Change doesn't cease because it's hard. Change isn't complete merely due to the discomfort of those who don't want to push for that additional rep. Change damn certain isn't about the approval of others who have been blocking the door.

Change isn't a compromise because it seems impossible. Change isn't about how we started out only able to do "one push-up," and now that we can do ten, we are done. Change pushes us to new levels, higher heights, farther distances, more intricate moves, incorporating more areas of the body... muscles we didn't even realize existed in this "body" of society.

And yes, you will eventually run up on someone who is "super serious" about this workout, with a transformative mindset... and they will be "no damn joke." They will demonstrate to you all the areas that are being neglected, underestimated, left out of the larger equation. You will feel like you have done nothing because change, just like working out, spans physical, mental, and spiritual aspects of our lives, pulling back layer after layer to get to root causes.

Change doesn't have a finish line. This workout is for life.

So, the next time you venture to say you wish people could just get along, that we should just stop talking about racism, hate, ignorance, violence, bigotry, prejudice, oppression, barriers, discrimination, white supremacy, false narratives, fragility, mental colonization, systemic policies, practices, procedures, biased laws, economic disenfranchisement, political marginalization, educational suppression, disparaging culture, historical pillaging, outright lies, entitlement, classism, superiority complexes, micro-aggression, macro-aggression, privilege... the list goes on...

...Yeah, change is a continuum, and it doesn't simply stop because things are so-called better than they "used to be." You don't get to determine that for Us. Because some of us are showing up every day in the gym of life, putting in those reps, adding weight, tacking on another half-mile, doing an additional lap, jumping that rope, practicing our bob and weave, counting steps, working the box, pushing for just one more, and another, and another.

Because change, whether you are for it or against it, is about our lives, our children's lives, our grandchildren's lives, our ancestors' sacrifices... just for us to be here. So, yeah, we are super serious about this mission. It is the only reason we are willing and able to stand here before you today. And that might just be a little too much for you to comprehend. We get it: you cannot wrap your head around "why" these folks won't just play along, get along, and make this all feel comfortable for you. Spoiler alert, it's not about you.

We'll let you in on a little secret: *not one day have we ever been truly comfortable in our entire lives* in this societal construct of racism. Because it was never meant for us to be accepted for who we are in this reality... you want us to accept things as they are. This reality was built on a model that didn't consider us human, worthy, or equal. It did not want to share, include us, or give us a power seat at the table... it just DIDN'T CONSIDER US at all. And now, we are here, wanting this nation to live out, in totality, fulfilling the words and ideals of freedom, justice, equality, liberty, the right to pursue happiness based upon an undeniable truth: ALL PEOPLE are created equal and have a RIGHT to that basic principle of humanity.

That's our workout every single day, and that's the mission... just in case you couldn't read between the lines of our analogous radical workout.

Get radical about something or be radically nothing.

|| Power of Black Love ||

Advocacy for all of humanity.

Dr. Cornel West[5] provides a beautiful explanation of Black Love in the learning series hosted on a Masterclass course titled Black History Freedom & Love[6]. The definition he provides expresses how Black Love can empower and save all of humanity.

As is my custom, I encourage everyone to delve deeper and explore for themselves, expanding our definitions and critically examining the world around us. Through study and learning, we broaden our knowledge base and leverage it to expand our perspectives. However, I will provide a summary with my takeaways from Dr. West's explanation of Black Love. Please take the time to explore it further for yourself.

Dr. Cornel West describes Black Love as an expressed journey to learn, care, and grow in understanding each person's connection to life, the world around us, and humanity. It is recognizing our sublime oneness with all things, an expansive connectivity to, nature, history, culture, and life. Black Love is unique in its ability to endure hardships, pain, persecution,

---

[5] http://www.cornelwest.com/
[6] https://www.masterclass.com/classes/black-history-black-freedom-and-black-love

brutality, and violence, while continuously emerging from trials and tribulations to challenge people to become better humans.

Black Love is empowering—not because it is exclusive to Black people but because it champions the highest levels of our humanity, stimulating people to endeavor to uphold what we say we believe in: the pursuit of happiness and liberty. Black Love calls us not just to be believers but livers of truth, through actions, deeds, ways of doing, and behaviors. It is the authentic knowledge that all people are created equal, that all people have a divine right to life, expression, and authenticity, and that all people have inalienable rights to be free, uninhibited by racism, hate, and ignorance.

If we would only sincerely embrace these concepts and ways of living, we will advance the human family to be fully inclusive in life, equitable towards all, not just in our lives, but beyond, with a true sense of belonging, creating a world that openly embraces diversity. If only we could pull ourselves up, stop stumbling over selfishness and narrow-mindedness in pursuing lies of exulted status, and stop selfishly believing in twisted concepts that some are destined to rule over others and possess all material things offered.

See, people fear Black... because they cannot understand true love. So many worry about dominance, that they cannot believe Black people will not reciprocate all the wickedness inflicted over the centuries upon those who have reaped the legacy of systemic despotism throughout the world. Yet, true Black Love is community a with fellowship for all people, forgiveness and that compels us all to evolve beyond a petty, childish vision of humanity and life.

Hate is nothing but a mask of fear. Let's choose to embrace Black Love. Being thankful for another day, even the challenging ones.

|| Open to Failure ||

Fear holds us captive.

We have an obligation to make our world a better place, emergent with better circumstances and conditions for humanity. We must stop looking for heroes/heroines and leaders to literally do the work for us, requiring them to grab us by the hand and drag us while showing the way. We have had a ton of heroes/heroines and leaders blaze trails, shine lights, paint visions, and espouse clear dreams for us to aspire toward. Yet, we wait. Waiting as if left in darkness. Waiting for what? Sacrifices have already been made.

It is time, my friends, to be about the work. Perfectionism is a fool's errand. We've been stubborn, stiff-necked and rebellious, standing upon shorelines of change, refusing to take one step forward to embrace the whirlwind. Indecisive, looking for someone to strike a staff of truth, opening pathways through seas of lies, falsehoods, and deceptions. Reality, educating ourselves through critical thinking, research, inspecting mission statements, plans, and calls to arise to the occasions are all vested for us to grasp. There is no more need for martyrs. The time is now for each of us to do our part, to make sorely needed changes as individuals, collectively, and as a nation, to advance the mission for bona fide inclusive democracy.

Our current sojourn calls to mind the story of Preacher Man. Preacher Man claimed faithful service to the cause, always advocating the power of inner connection to divine spirituality and how it manifested in our works within our world. As with all great claims of "faith," we shall be tested. The same is true for our commitment to liberate our hearts and minds from ignorance, hatred, racism, and mental oppression.

A brief cover of Preacher Man.

A terrible storm with flood waters was forecast

to directly impact the town Preacher Man lived in. Authorities went about the business of notifying residents on preparedness measures for evacuation. When authorities arrived at Preacher Man's home to make sure he was notified, as well as taking steps in preparation for evacuation, Preacher Man pronounced in an exalted tone, "My God will protect and deliver me." The authorities looked at one another, knowing that they wouldn't be able to sway Preacher Man in his stance.

As the storm began to materialize, dark clouds, high winds, and hard rain battered the small town. Authorities traversed town in an off-road vehicle, checking homes to ensure everyone had evacuated. To no surprise of the authorities, Preacher Man stood on the front porch of his home. Authorities waved him over. Again, Preacher Man announced, "My God will protect and deliver me."

Water started to rapidly flood the town, filling all streets and roads. Authorities came through in a boat, checking the community for people who were trapped, to evacuate. Yet again, they went by Preacher Man's home, hoping to reason with him on the necessity to leave. Once more, Preacher Man announced, "My God will protect and deliver me."

The storm escalated. Authorities came through the community one last time in a helicopter in an effort to save Preacher Man. The flood waters had engulfed the entire town. Authorities saw Preacher Man stranded upon the roof of his home. The authorities flew overhead, using a megaphone to call down to Preacher Man, imploring him to depart with them. Preacher Man stood up, bracing himself against the chimney and looking up, fighting high winds. Preacher Man began to say, "My God will protect and—' but was cut short by a torrential wave that arched high over Preacher Man's home, sweeping him away. The authorities' heads drooped, realizing in these weather conditions that they had no chance of finding Preacher Man.

A few eternal moments later, Preacher Man found himself in an intensely brightly lit space, waiting in line. Preacher Man was highly agitated and anxious. Preacher Man saw a being that seemed to oversee the flow of the line, directing people to chambers at the head of it. Preacher Man stopped the being and started to introduce himself. The being, that seemed to radiate light as it spoke, said, "We know who you are, Preacher Man." Preacher Man said, "I need to get to the head of the line; I have been a faithful servant, and I am really perplexed why I am here."

The being's energy seemed to nod along reassuringly. Then it said, "Of course, Preacher Man, we'll get you in immediately." The being escorted Preacher Man into a very large chamber. Preacher Man paced back and forth. Suddenly, the chamber seemed to fill with light and dark energy that flowed throughout with an intensity point at its center. Preacher Man heard his name echo through the chamber. Preacher Man stood erect, shoulders back, and began to express his frustration. Preacher Man accounted all the years of faithful service to the mission and cause through advocacy. The voice responded with energy that seemed to flow through the entire room all at once. "Yes, Preacher Man, all true."

Preacher Man went on. "Then I just don't understand it. When this storm came, why didn't you 'Protect and deliver me'?" There was a long-extended silence; the energy in the room seemed to ebb and flow, intensely bright and dark at the same time. Then, as if all at once from all points at once, the voice pronounced, "Preacher Man, who do you think sent the authorities to your home? Then the off-road vehicle? The boat? The helicopter? And finally, the wave? Preacher Man, in all your faith, you came to a point of expectation that deliverance required no effort whatsoever of you."

Then the room fell silent, and the energy departed.

This story's moral and principle is that we are all the Preacher. We as individuals, as a people and nation, have had many heroes/heroines and leaders sent unto us, standing before us, calling us toward higher ideals than the lived circumstances of time, imploring us to take up the work to change our world for a better humanity. And we have refused to take two steps forward, in effort and service, to work through adversity to make a difference in the world. We have arrogantly turned away, exclaiming it's someone else's responsibility to protect and deliver us. We have stood in silence as leaders have been struck down in their efforts to champion us. And, as we stand before opportunities and efforts to deliver us, we refuse, are dismissive, and turn away from the very tools sent unto us in the face of persecution, hardship, and captive state of triple darkness (blind, deaf & dumb) – ignorance. We expect an exalted path of perfection to be laid before us.

So, what shall it take, my friends? A final mighty wave of hate, ignorance, and racism to come along and sweep us away? Or will we embrace the mission that has been long advocated to advance true inclusive democracy for the entire human family through positive disruption, progressive change, social justice, and equitable access to resources, while developing a sense of belonging throughout communities? We can constructively improve people's lives, our larger society, future generations, and the world by mobilizing around "good trouble." You don't have to be a preacher to spread and live in truth, striving for righteousness, caring, and compassion. All you must do is pick up the burden you have been avoiding and lean into the work of change!

|| Dominant Culture Ain't My Vibe ||

Dominant culture is a mindset.

A framework of thinking that propagates values, language, standards, social strata, specific religions, beliefs, and behaviors as superior through imposed cultural, economic, and political power dominance dynamics...is a cultural mindset geared to control and require conformance against the true nature of humanity. A mental model designed in a way with expectations that everyone must conform to predefined roles is the undercurrent. A blueprint enforced by way of mechanisms, procedures, statutes, contrived laws, entertainment content... propagating "a right way" to further support assimilation by integrating a single standard into all facets of societal structures.... to sustain and maintain, a racial caste and class system at play set in motion through acts of violence, brutality, conquest, pillaging, and distorted narratives of hate. Dominant culture is steeped in rulership, not genuine leadership that inspires through noble purpose, energizes, nor empowers. It uses the terms, but it is subjectively applied to some people, not all people.

And when we the people raise a voice or protest to shift the narrative or implore abandonment of these suppressive philosophies and systemic practices that are so deeply interwoven throughout the fabric of our nation, we are labeled radical, angry, disruptors, rebellious, anti-this, anti-that, to silence and discredit segments of the population, a continuance to deny full representation within the nation while simultaneously devaluing our humanity for generations to come...

To bear witness, there are fundamental flaws, gaps in the economic capitalist system to "always" produce extreme disparities of haves and have-nots... as well as exploitation laced throughout all components of the political system, executive branch, legislative, judicial... an absolute failure to advance ideals of basic humanity...

There comes a time, a repulsion and compulsion to constructively yet radically disrupt the status quos embedded in our political patterns of behavior and practices. To shift the equation of disproportionate monopoly of power and resources... To cease the regenerative breath invigorating systemic injustices, void of moral fortitude to substantively address inequities and inhumanity... it must be openly acknowledged and confronted....and changed.

Mere displays of incremental token advancements to claim things are better are not substance. We continue to falter in addressing real disparities of livable wages, healthcare, food security, affordable housing, adequate public transportation, effective education, access to resources, and inclusive representation through all levels of government to be truly responsive to people's needs, not special interest or corporate interest. This is where we see dominant culture clutch up, again and again, intentionally blocking out, centering with indignation and audacity to claim reverse racism and discrimination. It is outright ludicrous, while failing to elevate or evolve in our Humanity as a whole.

This mind and system of rulership is self-destructive, thriving on suffering to extract capital by any means necessary—an absolute stranglehold on humanity's ability to advance and expand beyond gathering of material possessions. Dominant culture works to systematically eradicate the life source of humanity... it is no longer confined to the color of one's skin but a mindset of indoctrination, division, occupation, colonization, and ruling classes.

This is the truth of what America has become but not what it has to be limited to *being*... it is the truth of what we have settled upon, in our refusal to strive onward and upward in efforts to raise our ideals beyond petty catch phrases. We must be steeped in the principal knowledge that all people are created equal... Despite the inability of so-called leadership to uphold the core principle of all humanity is created equal. We must revolutionize our nation's mindset beyond race, dominance, and rulership. We must sincerely strive with a commitment to higher moral purpose to champion Humanity.

Until then, dominant culture is antithesis to my vibe.

|| Crabs Atop a Stool ||

Shoving others down.

We remain so divided as human beings, stagnating upon the concept that to be inclusive means loss. We are so fearful of openly sharing, embracing, having to work a little harder to consider other people who may look, act, pray, live, and/or love differently than we do. People claiming such things really do not exist... exist in a way that "they" should not be considered—that it is an antiquated form of thinking. Additionally, there is a momentum centered upon banning books that exam historical factors and events, the foundational blocks from which our nation sprang. We shun scientific rigor, reverting to base superstition, fanaticism, and spookism.

We dismiss how our society developed, was built, the core components for which it flourished. These same elements are woven into our culture, classism, political structure, economic design, and government modus operandi. Still, we claim history and science have no relevant bearing upon today's reality. We feign ignorance of the seed from which the tree sprang, denying that the fruits are ultimate products of those seeds. So much energy expended day in, day out, for hundreds and thousands of years, to suppress truth.

And for what? Because segments of the population do not have the moral capacity to digest and comprehend the legacy, the wake, resonating throughout our world. No, we would rather ban books, gut advocacy, arrest protesters, extinguish critical thinking and teaching, and scuttle research and analysis. We even distort facts, brushing them aside as fake news because they expose our inability to intelligently support or present informed counter positions of thinking. Simply because we cannot summon faith the size of a mustard seed to face harsh truths, learn and strive to do better. Ironically, we claim to be a spiritual nation, people of faith, champions of justice, fighters for freedom and liberty. As we bludgeon the world around us with atrocity after atrocity.

Such a sad contradiction we are, circling round, all to avoid open discourse, investigation of facts, and exploring ways to move beyond a racialist way of doing, to be better, to become better. We are like crabs atop a stool, fearful that someone else may knock us from our fragile perch. We would much rather run the risk of the stool toppling altogether before making space or a place for our fellow human beings. And that's why racism is real, breathing, and spreading at a high rate of speed. Steeped in fear.

Because of how hard you fight to conceal it, allege it has no relevance, it is all in the past. If this were so, a sophisticated examination of a nation's allegation of pulling themselves up by their bootstraps would not expose complete denial of a nation built upon the backs of so many human beings ground to dust while hoisting a jaded torch of liberty. If it were not all a lie, you wouldn't fight so hard to extinguish any and every voice that counters or opposes the regime's theme. The truth exposes contrarian actions and deeds.

We know you want to believe that it all sprang forth from an equitable playing field that was not founded upon entrenched racism. Yet, you contort when endeavoring to smother the truth of history. We know your name, babe of lies and deception. We know your ways, as demonstrated round and round the clock of time. Going to and fro throughout the land, seeking that which you can devour with your infectious hate and division of all those you encounter, consuming with your vile ways of oppression, your burden of denial, your yoke, as you stand upon the stool as a mighty crab, ensuring none shall surpass your limited construct of life, purpose, and being.

It is time to break free, my friends... step into the light, and shine radiantly bright.

|| African American or Black? ||

Am I African American or Black? What does it mean to subscribe to one, the other, or both?

I am not certain. I have listened and read through the swell...the discussion seems so reminiscent of debates I read about that transpired decades, perhaps eons ago. To be Calmly, Black, Negro, Afro, to be Super Black, and so much more.

What is lost in the discussion...We all are striving and aspiring to reclaim something stolen long ago: our true identities as a people. We can trace to the Middle Passage; some are fortunate enough to find scant details connecting directly to the continent, the Motherland of all humanity. Others leverage genealogy to find a connection via DNA...it is in my DNA family...not that hypocritical shit, the sucker shit of "the hypocrite in my DNA." Yeah, yeah, I get it. And truth, the history of bondage, who flipped on whom to be sold into the bowels of traders' ships chained into a nightmare reality of chattel existence. So, yes, the dilemma is real...What else is real is the choice between "to be Black or be African American." Why not all that and then so much more?

Both communicate incredibly significant points and meanings. African American acknowledges our ancestral connection spans beyond the United States of America while noting our people's history that bled into the oceans, seeped deep into the soil of this fledgling nation, helping it grow and accomplish in less than a century what required ages of other empires. It also pointedly calls for us to raise the fact that many African tribes, though a collective people, have distinct heritages and cultures that the slave trade disrupted and, in many cases, destroyed through the Middle Passage and the breaking process used to sever the lines of culture, heritage, language, religion, literature, accomplishments and ultimately, identity.

In turn, this is why I can embrace being Black as well...A love embrace and binding tie to Black consciousness and being. As we grow in awareness of the devastating impact of bondage and slavery...beginning to recognize the majesty and power of a people who have survived violence unparalleled throughout history and time. None have been held in such a brutal form of bondage and chattel servitude for so many damn centuries; none has the world so universally pillaged, raped, robbed, and despised. Yet here we are...Yes, damn it, here we are!

So, as we elevate in Black consciousness, we become aware, grow, nurture, and learn about us as a people—all our beautiful hues, shapes, forms, features, and styles. That we are unique in a multitude of ways, strong, independent, and expansively loving spirits as people. And we do not all shine black as mahogany. We span the spectrum array of beautifully Black shades down to the palest fragility. Yet, we are BLACK, no matter the situation or time of day... This is not about race for us, it is about a consciousness and awareness that amplifies our ones with the essences of All Life, moving in and out of Darkness, as that first spark and light of the eternal... quantum entanglement of all paths and dimensions without measure.

You cannot turn it off, you cannot code-switch your way out of it...nor should you fight it. Try as you might, though you are super light, Black child, you may as well have been born in the Congo at midnight. Because though it is no longer spoken, one drop of that blood makes you a Black folk, as justification to be amongst hated folk...as you strut around acting like you are a lily folk. So, save it with the switch-out artist flava, trying to cover your vibe and bop behavior. Black-ass joker, please... We see you upon your knees kissing up to what you perceive as closest to closest proximity.

Truth is, little sunshine, once they see how those sun rays dance around your super light gaze, as you brown up standing in the shade...you are Black, baby. Because you ain't their baby, even if claimed as a maybe, you ain't a white baby. So, do you, Boo. Talk the talk, walk the walk...I see you, watermelon man, once they hear about your background. Try as you might, baby, you cannot turn that round. Hell, you cannot even give it away. See, even if your MaMa is a white girl, she can leave you on the steps of an orphanage or even your great auntie's porch with a tear in her eye. She can go back, and just like that. For her, it's all about choices, on the other side of that hand, you cannot choose your way out of being Black, trying with all your might, even if you pass yourself off as white. Blackness will twist and tryst as you run about talking through your nose, dressing like the Bekah's and so-in-so's.

Black as the essence of night moving across the depths of the seas of light. Black as a child playing in the streets of any ghetto, hood, bayou, country road, dirt road, bush, or country club...thy Blackness leaps into the sky at night, spanning across the vast primordial waters of the heavens of universal light—Black and beautifully free, that first spark of life that set all things in motion...to be. That is as Black as you can be.

That is, you, baby, Black as you can be. Black is beautiful. Can you not see who you truly must be?

|| As We Judge ||

When people think they are above while placing others below.

As we look down upon complexion, nationality, gender, gender orientation, non-binary proscribing individuals, social status, racial categories, class, the educated or uneducated, those who have or haven't served, those with physical differences we deem disabilities, those with diverse mental capabilities, the young and the old, the religious and the non-religious...for all we justify categorization of other human beings as less than or beyond...these strained statuses, spun 'round to contrive degrees of superiority based on the twisted lust in our hearts, though we cannot prove the degrees we use to separate us a part...it's a masterful play, a character in the tragedy to advocacy for hate separating and splintering us apart, the hate that devils birth in people's hearts...against these others we use arbitrary measures to shuffle and sort us further apart...we stand in testimony, judging, reflecting the lack of empathetic hearts. Our lack is what truly sets us apart—an inability to understand humanity through the depths of a human heart. We squabble, degenerating our thinking, believing we make ourselves better at some other rate...but what truly is up for debate...who is the true degenerate as you spew your hate?

|| Battles ||

Choose them wisely.

Do not expend your energy on every trash-minded racist colonizer. Right, wrong, or indifferent, the ignorant play their part.

Keeping us distracted with fighting racism and hate making us do the work to help them educate, channeling our energy away from developing creative and innovative ways of expanding our humanity as they stand by caught in a disgusted gaze. It is all a distraction to force failure on broader and more important fronts. That is mission central for racist bigots. Summary failure to advance...it is not by happenstance.

|| Chasing Mainstream ||

Do not worry about finding stride within narrow minds, profiles societal standards always drowning in envy and lust. This life is so much more than the trifling categories they have combined...manufactured with carbon copies of falsehoods and lies, a disguise for superficiality as material tarts. Hell, they will tell you the sky ain't blue, same as the color in their lying eyes as they do, while trying to subdue you.

Break bad, so you can be you! Later, as you are reflecting back on yourself, you'll recognize it was nothing more than a sham leading down an ashen path that ends up in worship to a hippie boy, looking like a broken goldilocks' boy toy.

Celebrate your unique beauty, amplify thy distinguish-ness, thy beauty and finesse, even as they protest. All this life is about putting one to the test...but if you know what is best, love thyself, and do not give two hells about the rest.

‖ Playing It Safe ‖

Is fear.

I have found myself in conversations with people who seem impressed by what they consider my courage in using my voice to speak truth to people in positions of power or sharing my writings. What strikes me is that they think it is something unique that I somehow possess. If we have time, I strive to impart to them that there is nothing courageous, unique, or significant about what I am doing. Speaking up for what is obvious or true—there is nothing special about what I do.

Please do not misconstrue the comparison of the people I am about to name. If anything, I want to draw attention to the strength in their examples and sacrifices. While not attempting to take anything from them, understand they were all people, just like you and me.

Dr. Martin Luther King, Jr., El Hajj El Malik Shabazz (formerly known as Malcolm X), Sojourner Truth, Frederick Douglass, W.E.B. Du Bois, Harriet Tubman, Rosa Parks, Nelson Mandela, Steve Biko, Medgar Evers, Thurgood Marshall, James Baldwin, Huey P. Newton, Harvey Milk, and so many more known and unknown.

They all, one day, through either a series of events or a catalytic event, decided to raise their heads, their voices, their pens, their hands, or their fists. Something, at some point, resonated deep within their hearts, saying, "I will no longer remain silent, no longer go along to get along, no longer conform to the status quo, I will no longer..." And just like that, it started motion to go against a current that seemed insurmountable to so many others.

And I imagine the same is true of some soul, toiling away under the lash somewhere on some island or continent, in some field—a mere hundred years ago—raised their head up to wipe the sweat, blood, and tears from their cheek or brow, saying, "This cannot be the meaning of this life, this cannot be the place I am supposed to remain, this cannot be the sum of my existence nor the place of existence for generations to come. It isn't okay that I am treated worse than an animal, treated like chattel, denied basic humanity, denied opportunities, denied choices, denied human rights, denied dignity, denied, denied, denied... where others can indiscriminately, by will or whim, beat, murder, rape, take, pillage, hang, rob, abuse, mistreat, and use us as they wish. How are they morally better, sanctified, anointed, endowed by alleged righteousness bequeathed by a claimed merciful god to hold this place and position with us in bondage and a boot upon our necks? What makes them so superior because they, damn say so? Or is it due to their willingness to commit such heinous acts against other human beings?"

It just does not make sense; it doesn't add up, and those experiences go against every fiber of our being at some point, at some moment. And internally, it was decided to get up, stand up, speak up, run away, sabotage, foil, spoil, burn, push back, resist, and fight, by any means necessary. Even when the odds seemed insurmountable, we decided, "No more." With that came fear, I know for certain. We don't stay in that fear; we don't allow the fear to freeze us; we don't allow the fear to consume us... eventually, we embraced the fear to take a step forward, take a chance, to risk it, to strike out, to run, to hide, to sing, placing it all on the line, to dare, to desire more in this life, not going for the lie of "by and by, in the sky," waiting for the next life to be treated with dignity, respect, and humanity. We step through our fears!

And so, every time someone attempts to cast me as being brave or courageous, I stop them... to hopefully let them see and understand that it is so much more and bigger than I. Reminding them of all the blood, toil, and sacrifice, so many before me whom I pale in comparison to if weighed in the balance.

I am no hero; I am no martyr; I am not brave; I am truly not fearless. I just decided to raise my head up, wiping the toil from my brow, wiping the last tear from my eye, saying, "Enough." Because if I were to place my head back down, my soul would die a thousand times over. Just to hold a title, to have a job, to be invited into certain circles, to accept a wage, to have a place I am required to stay in, to hold on to the lowest rung in the societal caste system, to have so-called safety and security... at what cost? What do I have to give up? How many times do I have to deny that inner voice telling me this is not right? An ungodly reason I should be okay with a false narrative that some segment of the human family is entitled to rule over all others...? How many times do we compromise and sell our souls just to be accepted, to be slightly above others, a token, coveting a place at the feet of a throne built upon the backs of Indigenous people, to live confined within terms outlined by others? How damn many times?

There is not anything special about finally recognizing that if we think it isn't right, unfair, unjust, biased, broken, and doesn't consider all of us as human beings. That is not special. We make it special because we acquiesce our power by continuing to submit to fear. I have risked my life for unworthy causes a hundred times over on and in the block. Now, all I am doing is hoping to strike a spark for something so much more worthy/noble than I, to shine a light and pray it vibrates, rippling to reach many more to disrupt and radically change the world for the better... which requires all of us to eventually step toward our fears and walk through them, being about the work, thoughts, actions, and deeds to make this world a better place for all of humanity.

I see you, my friends. Step forward; it is time.

‖ Hey, DEIB... How are You Doing? ‖

If you cannot fathom how diversity, equity, inclusion, and

belonging (DEIB) are connected to how you treat, respond to, think of, and interact with individuals—team members, departmentally, organizationally, neighbors, community, and nationally—how can you fix your face to claim being a catalyst for change? Systems changing ultimately requires working as a collective, in community, in partnership, to authentically disrupt for societal good in solving the gaps, disparities, and inequities, such as, but not limited to, food insecurity, affordable housing, health care, education, thriving wages, adequate transportation, representation, access, human rights, and so much more to uplift our humanity. Not just serving people in lines of need. That is not change, that is maintaining the same status quo, and outcomes.

Systems change is not limited to projects and programmatic work, policies, and organizations you support. It is about our habits, behaviors, practices, thoughts, and decisions, interwoven at the very base level of how we treat people. How do you support the work when you engage people with a mindset of rulership, a savior mentality, a holier than thou mind, from a lofty perch of false superiority? Why, because you claim to be a good person? Is good really limited to a narrow aspect of your life? We intend to topple that garbage in all forms, in all capacities, spaces, places, every slanted decision and inequitable outcome while you dare claim your voice is advocacy, dismissing DEIB as not being mission critical... Damn, you are so hypocritical.

It is so much more than taking a damn training course or using an equity tool or mechanism. It is about our lived behaviors and our collective actions and connection to other human beings in this life. It is a personal journey at so many levels, and yes, the work and the mission. Failure to embrace it, live it, breathe it, be it, tarnishes the impacts, outcomes, and results by-way of all those incidents where you mistreated your colleagues who happen to be neighbors, community members, and the people we raise up, claiming to be in the mission to serve. So, without an evolution of our thinking moving beyond our sanctimonious sackcloth, self-righteous savior crap... we all fall short in noble mission and purpose to uplift humanity.

Step down off that delusional pedestal and walk amongst the true and living—thy neighbors.

|| Turbulence ||

Good morning, folks, the captain has advised there's turbulence ahead. So, if you are not strapped in, please do so before reading any further. We ensure the ride is about to get rough, so for your safety, we have instructed the crew to cease providing amenities.

A team, organization, community, social dynamic, and nation comprises a cumulative reflection of what the people demonstrate not just in words but/and deeds.

We hear a lot about how great our nation is or was since some folks think we need a few retakes. In this case, I am referring to the United States of America. I personally must recognize many of the opportunities I have experienced in life are related to the country I was born in. And for those of you who have secretly wondered where that may be because of my name, yes, it was the USA. In fact, Washington, D.C., our nation's capital. So, yes, I understand I have been afforded many privileges that are not readily available in other nation-states.

The thing that stands out to me, though, is that people want to talk about how great our nation is or should be. A whole segment of the population does not want to teach, review, discuss, nor learn from our nation's history. They fear it will make some people uncomfortable while piping off at the mouth about how great we are as a nation. In what context, since we are attempting to deny the history that contributed to where we are today? At what point do you think it is okay to discuss our nation's history? Fifty years ago? 60, 100, 200? What is comfortable to you?

Think about that. If a potential applicant/candidate wanted to join our company or team, we would want to "know more about their background," right? Yet, we dare not discuss the history or background of our nation, events, phases, trials, tribulations, struggles, sacrifice, and efforts from all people who have contributed to this nation's becoming. We want to shy away from the ups, downs, and painful experiences.

Really? Because it will make some folks uncomfortable? You might as well say we do not want it taught to school-age children. Oh damn, that's right forgot about Florida. We have the audacity to call our schools institutions of learning. Give me a break; we cannot be the home of the brave while being suspended in fear of teaching the real nitty-gritty of our nation's path to where we are today. It is like waking up on a trail deep in a forest without any idea of where you started nor where you intend to head. Guess what it results in? Wandering in the wilderness, back tracking and retracking areas you have been...cannot enter the promised land if while in the wilderness of rebelliousness you have no idea or direction on the "why" and "how" you got here so you can determine what direction is forward.

We have trolls in the legislative branch, judicial, executive houses, corporate executive offices, boards of directors' room, trillionaire idiot clubs thinking they are geniuses on every topic beyond the scope of what they have accomplished, in school board meetings, boasting things like this nation was single-handedly built by a specific group of people... Basically white folk claiming they did it all by themselves. Lying about our nation's past and extolling warped concepts of how freaking awesome we are as if some great gift to the world. Then specifically tagging everyone throughout the world to look upon us in amazement of our greatness while being certain to leave out anything and everything crappy committed throughout time or that was not our finest hour.

And we sit center stage with our fingers crossed on being

almost famous. We raise ourselves as a pillar and example to the world around. Yet, we refuse to talk about our past, its context, those hard patches, or any not-so-proud moments.

We are living a lie. We attack anyone and everyone with a counter narrative with absurd made-up events, distorting facts, fabricating outcomes, and finally inciting violence when people demonstrate and disprove our lies. Then we ironically call it a cancel culture while cancelling the entire legacy and truth of the blood trail to our current nation's status. I am sorry you might have to answer a couple of tough questions. That should not be a problem. You claim to be a hard-ass, and so-so damn smart, don't you?

We lack virtue in examining our nation's history to hopefully garner deeper insights through a growth mindset, raising up ideals that have yet to be fully applied in actions and deeds does not mean those ideals should be limited by the minds of men and their times. It is time to develop a serious cadence of learning that can be curated from our history.

We are ignoring the blood that birthed US... This is us, and we are doing this at every level throughout our nation: local, state, on hills and benches of the highest order in the land and world around. We seem to lack the aptitude to acknowledge our nation's history. Yet, we arrogantly point out others should be able to do better. I honestly think as a nation-state, we do not even understand the definition of "great" if we are so skittish about our nation's evolution. So, next round, miss me with that crap if you don't want to talk, Real Talk.

If you are wondering. Yes, I think the United States of America has done many remarkable things. Though there are numerous periods when we failed on all counts, this does not mean throwing the baby out with the bath water. We do not need to burn it down. But it does mean we have to grow stronger by unpacking the harsh reality, and we can only do this by starting to be honest with ourselves. That begins with learning and understanding our nation's full history, great portions, good, bad, ugly, and heinous periods.

Divided we shall fall.

We shall not advance nor truly prosper until we grapple with the truth of what racism and the hate it generates within the psyche of our nation. Our aversion to open discourse about ugly aspects of our nation is undercutting ascension above or beyond our limiting status quo. And until we somehow start to unpack the harm, how racism is enemy number one tearing us apart from within. We are one precipice of turning an even worse corner, a path that will make all the horrible crap look like a day trip down sunshine lane. If we cannot embrace change for salvation as a collective, as a fully inclusive, equitable representative nation rooted in our common humanity, we are on a fast track to destruction. Sitting in a metaphorical straw handbasket waiting at the brink and gates of Hell.

|| While We Bicker, Squabble, and Fight about Race ||

Oppression of the masses quietly marches forward.

Our histories are wrapped in racial division. While we squabble about racial matters, regardless of so-called genetic makeup, we as a human family are being slowly but surely subjugated. Racial matters are real, and big issues need to be thoughtfully dissected. People need to be educated on them, and some people need to be called out for straight racist thinking and practices, especially inequities leaning toward a culture built upon lies of contrived superiority. Still, this is not the true endgame for an elitist percentage of the population. As we focus on the present danger of racial class, caste, economic-strata and division, power brokers are hyper-focused on stripping basic citizen rights, squashing free thinking and free speech, and eradicating critical inspection by the masses.

Thus, we need to step back to contemplate this in-depth. As we are sucked into the rhetoric of demagoguery and distraction tactics regarding immigrants allegedly taking jobs (in many cases, ones we wouldn't consider doing), and claims that Blacks are out to reverse the roles of racism (just cite a few current Supreme Court decisions), all the while lapping up that hype, we are supporting people set on contriving positions of extreme power who are actively tearing away the rights of all of our citizenry.

We are supporting platforms driven towards suppressing education, undermining voting rights in the misguided interest of keeping out fraudulent votes, and dismissing critical inquiry with catchphrases, we are sacrificing freedom to snuff-out propped-up "enemies" driven by fearmongers. Basically, we are signing up and supporting the oppression of all people, and resigning the human family to a mindset of docile ignorance that can be exploited for generations to come. Power brokers want more power, and in many cases, are flunkies trying to get access to that upper 10% of extreme wealth and power. We are unwittingly facilitating our own manipulation through fear, selfishness, and ignorance, giving away the greatest pillar of power we hold, Independence of mind. We are knowingly and unknowingly aiding and abetting those who are intentionally stoking our differences as divisors, pitting us against other human beings. Our power as a collective is knowledge.

When we say we are uber-focused on social justice for our neighbors, community members, our nation, and the world, we must dive deep to ensure that as we strive for equitable processes, policies, practices, and behaviors, we aren't committing an eye-for-an-eye trespass. Diversity is more than counting outward appearances as a surface level of understanding; it includes diversity of thought—there is no standard operating procedure we can cascaded outward to navigate the pitfalls of centuries of inflicted pain. It requires authentic inclusion, even of those who may not seem real allies or not committed to a position of a shared future. There is strength and jewels of healing in healthy exploration, navigating extremely difficult and uncomfortable conversations, along with rigorous debate framed with good intent to seek out sincere understanding. That is building; that is a path towards belonging.

We do not have to agree on every point. For some reason, folks think it is an all-or-nothing type of deal. Yes, we do have to be about the work, coming from a real place, which is only shown and proved through the wisdom of our deeds. Yet, we will not walk nor channel through the same path centering upon 360 degrees of multi-dimensional Knowledge of Self.

Seeking out understanding is the best part.

|| Blood of Thy Path ||

What is thy vision if thou haveth no hope and what is hope without vision?

- ∞ We continue to stumble in ignorance because we do not want to accept the truth of our intertwined history.

- ∞ We continue to pursue hate because we do not want to acknowledge our silent consent to harm.

- ∞ We continue to shirk our duty because we do not want to work to build a cojoined humanity.

- ∞ We continue to accept loss of life by telling ourselves its they or them.

- ∞ We continue to support subjugation as matters of history as it is liters our modern systems.

- ∞ We continue to funnel bi-lateral support out of fear and recompense.

- ∞ We continue to bathe in blood of innocence, cloaked in

shrouded missions of good.

We shall not gain justice through our unjust means. We cannot claim moral high ground while our actions are of the most low.

There is no righteousness in our unrighteous deeds; there are no accolades for surrendering our souls to propagate pseudo-stature above claimed enemies.

There is only a gaping hole of loss, blood of regrets, with our hands soaked in futile virtue, alleged blessing of the Most-High.

It is past time to rise out of vomited filth, to be cleansed in compassion, strength, love, and tribulations to qualify our oneness with the Divine Essence of All Life.

> *"First, they came for the Communists*
> *And I did not speak out*
> *Because I was not a Communist*
> *Then they came for the Socialists*
> *And I did not speak out*
> *Because I was not a Socialist*
> *Then they came for the trade unionists*
> *And I did not speak out*
> *Because I was not a trade unionist*
> *Then they came for the Jews*
> *And I did not speak out*
> *Because I was not a Jew*
> *Then they came for me*
> *And there was no one left*
> *To speak out for me."*

—Pastor Martin Niemöller, First They Came (1946)

|| Casting Stones ||

The world will heap abuses upon us.

Life can be beautiful; life can be cruel.

This brings to mind a great fable about an ass that was scorned.

One day, along a stretch of road, a passerby noticed an ass that had fallen into a deep hole. The passerby mocked the animal, calling it cruel and disparaging names, stating how foolish the animal was to haphazardly fall into such condition. The passerby had no understanding as to why or how the ass had found itself in such a situation. Regardless, the passerby noted the ass's current circumstances proved it deserving. Before continuing their journey, the passerby cast a stone at the ass, striking it.

Another passerby came along, seeing the ass stuck in such a deep hole. The passerby considered the animal's situation, muttered how ignorant it was along with attached obscenities, shaking their head at its obvious stupidity. Again, before departing, the passerby picked up a stone, casting it, striking the animal for its shameful condition.

Then another passerby came, seeing the ass stuck in the hole. This passerby considered the ass's condition, brimming with advice shouting out what the animal should do. The ass did not respond nor take heed. The passerby pondered a little longer, becoming frustrated at the ass's inability to get out of the hole on its own accord. Eventually, in frustration, the passerby picked up a stone, casting it at the beast striking it harder than the previous passersby.

This scenario played out repeatedly, always ending with the passerby casting a stone at the ass. Until, one day, the ass nudged all those stones into a pile, climbing up the wall of the scornful condition it had found itself in. Finally, the ass walked out of that hole and went back about the work of its noble purpose.

I look at life's periods, where people will come along, gazing upon us as a troop of ass. They will have much to say about our condition, situation, and circumstances. They will have much advice, in most cases, casting judgmental stones based upon our current state as proof that we are not worthy. They will cast their stones again and again, striking us, and those stones shall hurt. Just as with the ass, all stones of judgment and condemnation will fall to our feet, and we will eventually gather those stones up, building a pathway out of our wretched circumstances. And, just as the ass, we, too, will walk out, to be about our true purpose. That noble purpose, in this case, within our inner heart and spirit—not what was determined by those who cast judgment upon us, striking us, inadvertently thinking of us as lowly and resigning us to such a despised station.

By each stone cast upon us, we shall gain an additional building block in the path to thee, Beloved.

|| Colonizer Frame of Mind ||

Not knowing you.

The cat's out of the bag. People are exposing lies strewn about, falsehoods interwoven throughout. And colonizers are beside themselves trying to control, contain, and maintain the narratives.

How dare the scourge of the earth teach history with a focus upon truth? The audacity! Outlining that there were no thanks given while pilgrims pillaged and stole land, only murderous deeds were bred by hands of the hidden thieves. Au contraire mon frère! Underserved tenaciously serving up accounts of systemic exploitation. Those uncivilized, unprofessional, unlearned so-and-so's breaking free from the mental strongholds.

Unless... wait a minute... can colonizers somehow monopolize and monetize Diversity, Equity, and Inclusion as an untapped stream of revenue? Oh, dang! Now you are cooking with grease baby—money is music to colonizer ears. Leverage the dominant machine, punishing those who do not toe the line of the party's rhetoric and line, to contribute to the capitalist scheme and machine. Everything has its price to some, consequently, so should everyone. Just identify their weakness, press it, forcing firebrands and magnets into a fold of sanctioned scripts. Wrangling in mindsets to ensure the colonizer's bidding remains predominant and core. And, at last, those who do not conform—pit them one against another. There can only be one or two head so-and-so's in charge, they are told and sold.

Auction block of certification, DEIB, as a profession. Capitalism strikes again.

|| Declare Thy Independence ||

We actually have a choice.

Declare independence from perpetuate hate, ignorance, falsehood, committing harm unto others, mean-spiritedness, being inconsiderate, arrogance, stereotypes, biased thoughts, bigotry, supporting suppressive cultural tropes, and behaviors of entitled self-promoting and warped agendas. Declare independence from discriminating against people based on race, gender, sexual orientation, creed, nationality, class, religion, mental and physical abilities, military service status, and the array of differences we possess as human beings.

Declare independence from imposing dominant cultural standards politically, socially, economically, educationally, and personally. Declare independence from going along to merely get along out of fear of being disruptive, radical, or making people feel uncomfortable about their complicit role extolling dominant socio-cultural frameworks.

Declare independence through conscious awareness, radically disrupting the root cause pillars of a caste system propagated through every vicissitude of our societal functions. Declare that we will follow through, day in and day out, with acts of kindness, thoughtfulness, caring, respect, dignity, considering potential impacts, through policy changes, procedures, practices, inactions, and actions that undermine our humanity. Declare to oppose the stranglehold racism has upon our world through distorted concepts of superiority over all other segments of the human family.

Declare independence by way of commitment to equitable access to education, learning, being informed, and freeing our minds from injustices, inequitable treatment, laws, and decisions that force people into caged definitions of being. Declare and dare to stand for liberation of our fellow human beings breaking yokes of suppression, repression, and oppression supported through our economic constructs feeding extremes and accepted gross disparities of resources within the "Land of the Free and Home of the Brave."

Declare independence and no longer merely claim we are for liberty. Let us declare *Liberty* through our demonstrated actions, deeds, ways of doing, and treatment toward all, moving beyond philosophical platitudes. Declare as our pledge and allegiance for which we stand as, "...one nation, indivisible, with liberty and justice for all," by demanding it in all aspects of life, with staunch advocacy and defense in real-world contexts and experiences, each day.

And when times get tough and challenging, we do not cower nor run off, shirking our duty, nor be found derelict in our commitment to uphold the inalienable right that all people are created equal. We must stand before the world, upholding these convictions as beacons of hope to protect the beauty and majesty of all human beings... this is a noble purpose my friends!

No more performative, outward, hollow words. Teach it, live it, and *Be It!*

|| We Know Deep Down We Can Do More ||

Nothing changes unless we put forth a greater opposing force.

"The language of soul. . . possesses a pronounced lyrical quality which is frequently incompatible to any music other than that ceaseless and relentlessly driving rhythm that flows from poignantly spent ideas."

**—Claude Brown,
author of *Manchild In the Promised Land***

We have an obligation as participants in human experience to listen to our hearts and spirits, being courageous in pursuing the notion that we can do better, not just one day but every day. Collectively, we can generate ideas, solutions, plans, pulling together the appropriate people to execute with clarity. We will hit barriers, we must adapt, we will problem-solve, stimulating emergent and innovative ways of doing as we overcome, burrow through, close gaps, forging paths, and building bridges forward—empowered and better because of it.

We must stop contemplating "what if" and instead imagine forward (*if*) followed with strategic actions. Or we shall look back with regret and shame as our narrative exposes us to generations to come that we failed to try harder, sacrifice, push more, risk more, dared to care, or step forward through our fears to courageously challenge the status quo. Do not forsake a higher calling of purpose as warrior for humanity.

Avoid being dominant culture's steppin' fetchin' hoe.

|| Defining Moments ||

"Life is not measured by the number of breaths we take but by the moments that take our breath away."

—1989 "Tahitian Choreographies"
by Vicki Corona

Defining moments can be positive experiences as well as traumatic ones. It is not what we may be experiencing that shapes us; it is how we navigate, work through, summon lessons, unpack wisdom, and apply to propel forward through those crucible moments which define aspects of who can *Become.*

Do not allow the moment to possess and obsess you. Show and prove by how you come out of them, along with the decisions and actions you take from there rising *Beyond them.*

|| Education and Learning ||

Saved my life.

Though I did not want to recognize it at an early age, pursuing education and the learning experiences along the way would save my life. My mother exposing me to various aspects of life, buttressed by Aunt Hannah's encouragement, and Aunt Ethel's fierce love throughout my younger years, instilled the significance that higher education, would eventually pay off. Little did I know that the ability to read and comprehend, and insights gained through understanding baselines sciences would help me weather storms in the darkest recesses. Several of those storms were self-inflicted growing up in D.C., Maryland, and Viriginia (now interestingly referred to as the DMV).

As I reflect back I believed I wouldn't live to see 21 years old and many close friends turned their backs (as I found out later, they confessed to thinking I wasn't going to survive that life), it was education and my passion for learning that I ultimately leaned upon. Education gave me rays of hope that something better awaited beyond the darkest periods and pockets of my life. When I was engulfed by violence, crews, gangs, murder, and double or triple crosses, the potential of getting life without increased with every ill decision, my love for learning turned out to be my redemption. The one thing I was embarrassed to share openly ended up illuminating a pathway out of an imposed and self-created hell.

Why would someone be ashamed of being able to read, write, comprehend, explain concepts, and unpack difficult topics in simple and organic ways? Basically, it wasn't cool, and I would end up in fights for being accused of trying to be "smart" again and damn again.

It was a mental and physical environment where trying to be so-called school "smart" was only accepted if you intended to leverage it to get over or take advantage of others, be conniving, or exploit—outside of that, it just wasn't cool. None of those characteristics really required one to be able to read, write, comprehend, understand scientific concepts, pursue an interest in technology, or possess a love for the sciences of life. So, I tucked those nuggets away as I adapted to the environment I perceived, taking on attributes necessary to survive, rolling hard in street life. And yes, I dove deep, on the rock-hard side of the pool. I went all in. This is what the world of notorious "they" said I should be, that was the realm of limits to thrive within. Or so I thought. In turn, I gave it my all.

As a teenager, I traversed the madness I invited into my life. Ironically, even within the depths of it all, I insisted upon going to school. None of my family members knew the ugly side of life I had chosen because I went to school full-time and maintained grades. I lived a dual life, secretly reading all kinds of books and learning about new tech while concealing it from the street side of who I was, and painstakingly making sure the street did not invade my home. My hyper-concern was one of the sides would blow up the fallacy of the other. You cannot keep it gangster while being viewed as a nerd reading books on computer engineering. That was weak. Nah, couldn't reveal taking computer programming nor engineering courses—it would have been exploited as being a sucker, soft, and a victim waiting to happen. That was life, defined by hard boundaries, rolling with a loose-knit crew.

The curiosity of learning would not leave me alone, though, even while standing on the block listening to guns blaze in the background, witnessing as we all compromised our hearts for a soulless existence. It was the words of my mother, Aunt Hannah, Aunt Ethel, and eventually my father that haunted and gnawed at me as I rode waves of destruction crashing down on our communities, one after another. And though I thrived in that pain and suffering, I would wonder, "Is this really all we are meant to be?" as I listened to my friends plotting on one another because one had access to a serious connect or just scored on a helluva robbery from the other side of town.

In the back of my mind, I mulled over the schemes, and double/triple crosses, wondering, "Damn, we used to ride bikes and play video games with this dude, and now you want to chop his head off for a couple of quarters in the scheme of things?" I really did not understand that you could not stand neck-deep in filth and avoid becoming corrupt too. That revelation came to me later one night as I found myself contemplating snuffing out one of my closest friends because he had crossed me on some petty street crap. Now my rep was potentially on the line, and I not only had to maintain that line but had to respond a hundred-fold to secure it so that all others would know my responses were extreme. That is how I held this lie together with all the f'ing characteristics of contradiction. As I sat there contemplating my next move, on one of my closest homies, who wasn't even aware that word had circled back to me on what he and his cousin had done to cross me (loyalty on the street is funny like that; money and threats of life and death make people do insanely stupid things), my inner voice spoke to me. I really did not give a damn about what "they" thought. I was struggling with the arbitrary lines I held, what I valued, what I perceived as trust, loyalty and love for my brothers, shit that I just would not do to people within "my circle" even with all the irony of the violent life we lived.

It was that day I realized how far I had allowed this street shit to pull me from my center—to one of the darkest points, weighing snuffing out the life of my friend, one of my closest friends, over what really amounted to a petty transgression in the scheme of things. A person I had laughed with as a kid, fought other kids with to get our stolen bicycles back, and committed to being there for one another, no matter what. Homies until the very end. Girls we met and hung out with, the eventual mothers of our children, though we were all kids ourselves. Jumping turnstiles at the subway station, sneaking through the back door of buses, hell hanging on the back of buses, rolling from one move to another, always trying to come up, thinking we were slicker than slick.

Now, I found myself wrestling with a decision, looking in a mirror, unable to recognize the person looking back at me, who I had become. That was the beginning of the end of my street life, though it was a long way from over. During that time, I realized I had become a person I was terrified of—someone I did not want to know and would be ashamed of. A person I never wanted my mother, Aunt Hannah, Aunt Ethel, or my father to meet in the raw on the street. A complete savage, ugly, calculating, and cold-hearted plotting two and three moves ahead just not to end up dead. The pain I had distributed block by block, one project after another, prying open doors of weakness, hood to hood... the lives I was snatching with shuttering heartbreak to my ancestors.

That is when I truly learned that there is always a choice in this life, even in our darkest moments. Life will bring cold realities to confront you one-on-one. No matter how you try to ignore the truth of who you are, what you could be versus what you have allowed yourself to become, you always have a choice. And it is your will and power to deny or refuse to accept the reality of every horrible step you have taken against your true purpose. Giving up on yourself is the worst thing you can ever do, even when the rest of the world seems to have turned its back on you, thinking you could not possibly survive or come out the other side wiser and stronger for the pain inflicted.

Regardless of the harsh judgment society spews upon you, those are moments that make it easy for others to universally dismiss you as a loser, unworthy, expendable, of no consequence in contributing to life... judging people as having no prospect of redemption, is the shallowest form of self-righteousness. Block out the noise, power it down, or literally throw it away. Step back and listen to that voice deep within your heart. Embrace the pain and heartache, listen, and know you too are worthy. Know that you have so much more to offer. Know that there is more to life than immediate circumstances and temporal conditions.

Listen to the yearning of your soul, calling you to walk away, to pivot hard, and seek something better. Believe and know there is so much more. You can grow; you can overcome; you can be a better version of you. That one moment or moments will not forever define you, even with blood on your hands. It will not be the end of you. You must learn how to love yourself, give yourself a chance, give yourself grace, give yourself forgiveness, because you are more than circumstances, a present that cannot comprehend your future if you only accept the strength and determination to step forward to the light and truth and fight like hell to be a better you. Just as hard has you grind on the streets...it's time to turn your hustle into striving for a better you every day, hustling, hustling, hard! Let's get it!

It is real, blood in, blood out, and it is a tragedy from every angle. Whether it is direct harm or harm vicariously by-way of proxy... it all sums up as senseless and unnecessary outcomes and loss. And this, too, shall pass. You can do this, my friend. You can carry this burden, and pay your penance in sacrifice, hard work, strength, and rough love. I know—I was there, in a box, real and imagined, at one time. We make our own cages too, and we can arise to a higher calling driven by a noble purpose... my friend.

‖ Energizing Aspect of Joy ‖

Think about what really energizes you, recharges you, and feeds your soul. Is it sharing concepts, ideas, learning, coaching, mentoring, partnering with people to navigate complex problems? Putting in hard work to clean up a vacant lot, renovate a building, give a speech to a group of people on a topic dear to your heart, or share details of experiencing vulnerabilities to grow stronger?

Is it participating in a consortium to exchange strategies on tackling profound questions, negotiating contract terms, sealing a deal? Or is it having one-on-one conversations related to social, political, cultural, or economic challenges and how we can work as a collective community to better address these broad, sweeping matters?

Or is it meditating in a quiet place, hiking a trail, rock climbing, cycling, jogging, lifting weights, prayer, yoga, racing motorcycles, reading an insightful book, tinkering with parts, restoring antique cars, building a website, recording a podcast, writing about uncomfortable topics, or tutoring?

Yeah, you're starting to get it. "IT" can be anything or several things, but you must listen, learn, and understand what energizes your inner heart, spirit, passion(s), and essence of being. And if you are fortunate enough to figure out what "IT" is, you have an obligation to identify ways to incorporate it into your life's journey in significant ways. When life reveals something beautiful to you from within and outwardly...it is a sin against your spirit not to reach for and pursuit with passion.

Why? Because it will power you forward in this life. Stop fearing that part of you, worrying that others will deem it foolish, uncool, goofy, or weird. IT is a part of your unique and beautiful self, and you must first embrace it to leverage and amplify your superpowers. It is your soil of enrichment, the water that revives you, the light that warms and sustains you through difficulty. It is what makes you grow, become stronger, and radiates that essential inner light for all the world to see. It is a part of your best self that you have been running from!

IT's that time... Dreamville, J. Cole[7] (warning: explicit lyrics).

‖ Hello, My Inner Faith ‖

I do not have all the answers nor profess to know the "right" way. However, I do sincerely advocate for a more inclusive, just, and equitable world for us to engage as human beings. By no means is there one perspective, or solution. It requires tactical efforts for us to grow and improve our communities. Yet, we must be willing to express our thoughts, ideas, contentions, and grievances in constructive ways, authentically and sincerely. In many cases, that requires us to openly express vulnerability. In doing so, we must know in our hearts that we are speaking or writing from a place of good intentions. Still, it is important to understand our message may not resonate and will cause discomfort for others, and that's okay. Growth towards our best selves is not an easy path.

Additionally, we must recognize as we look around our communities, regions, countries, and the world, that it is clear we are allowing ourselves to be polarized by differences that do not outweigh our fundamental connection as human beings. Yet, here we are, fighting about issues, processes, so-called norms, societal strata, systemic biases, and standards as if they mean

---

[7] https://www.youtube.com/watch?v=XrpPOtPHY_Y

more than the people they are being imposed upon. We need to understand and believe in the power and ability of people again. We need to be inspired by the potential of humanity rather than allowing the vicious actions of a few to become our looking glass for the rest of the world.

I did not always share my views openly. I tended to focus on doing me: studying, learning new things, improving my business skills and professionalism, and advancing my education. But as I continued to try to sidestep big issues in life in general, I questioned myself: What is the value of all these things? Was the goal simply to gather up as many jewels of knowledge as possible, or was I meant to leverage them to change my surroundings for the better? Did I foolishly believe I could exist in a world of hurt, trials, tribulations, and ignorance while remaining silent?

Then I look at my son and my daughter... I look back to all the people who took the time to help me, investing in a potential they saw within me that I did not perceive in myself. I think about my family members who had so many unrealized hopes and aspirations... and I recognize that I have a debt to repay and a responsibility to raise my voice. I must champion those who may not have the eloquent words or be able to speak up and those who do not have the luxury to share their message because they are actively being persecuted.

Now, do I necessarily think my words and efforts to support radical change go far and wide? No, they do not. I can do more, and I am willing to do more. This book is one of many steps to do more. But as some have mentioned this thought of "stability," and "comfort", these can be crosses to bare when you want to speak truth openly and especially when challenging those who believe they hold ultimate power. Not everyone will agree with or take kindly to it. And we must overcome fear and summon courage in our hearts and spirits to ask, "If not you, then who?" We must be willing to put in work and sacrifice at times, if we want to see a better world that is safe and inclusive for all human beings, regardless of their so-called station or stature in society. People are our greatest asset, and we need to be reminded of and demonstrate that every day... until compassion and caring are rolling down as thunderous waves of actions and deeds, everywhere, and without question.

With all that said, we must humbly work to bring people together to leverage our collective intelligence, resources, and efforts through noble purpose constructively serving our communities. And it starts first with everyone's commitment to positive impacts and outcomes. *Leadership means being driven in service of a mighty purpose, emanating from the depths of our hearts and spirits, guided by principles that transcend the individual and unite us as a collective.*

|| Four-Letter Word ||

Hope - /hōp/ (Google search)*

1. *a feeling of expectation and desire for a certain thing to happen.*

2. *a feeling of trust.*

Hope fosters determination: a determination to overcome circumstances, obstacles, set-backs, trials, and tribulations—our ability to be tenacious despite failures. We hold that power and channel it through our daily efforts to change the world around us based upon what we control from within. We do not acquiesce to hate, exclusion, nor persecution. Your privilege is a false cloak of power, while simultaneously it is our yoke of suppression. Hope shields us against your onslaught and thirst for blood. We see your fear in your murderous persecution. We recognize your insecurity about a world of diversity, equitable treatment, sincere inclusion, and the world being a place where we all belong.

Hope calls out whether you can achieve without entitlements, bias, discrimination, and systemic racial caste. Yes, our hope terrifies your place of unjust dominance. Yet, our hope does not imply nor mean reversal of roles to become oppressors of morrow. Our hope includes your presence and acceptance once you release your hate, distorted concepts of superiority and delusion of anointed dominance towards the entire human family. Our hope shall prevail, and your hate shall fail.

Watch us. Your vile words and deeds shall not stop us. Our hope shall press onward... as we bear witness to the truth, speaking it into existence through our supportive deeds. We hope for you, too, our self-appointed enemy, frail and insecure paper enemy. Soon, hope will embrace you as well, allowing you to recognize the truth of our hearts.... Hope will leave you no choice, no path forward other than to come forth into the light of humanity. Hope is not a nightmare... it is a vision just around that dark corner in your fear filled heart. Go on, take that next step.... Hope is waiting for you too. Summon that courage, release that fear, let go of foolish notions of elevated places over me, we. Hope shall be. And we all shall be free of the hate ailing our world.

Hope's got you.

|| Hot Mic ||

Hearing private conversations.

We are always on point. We speak our truth, not when it is convenient, comfortable, or accommodating by a predetermined schedule. We live it—like hype—stick and shield as we walk through life... Warriors' life, 24/7, elevated through 360 degrees: 120 degrees knowledge, 120 degrees wisdom, 120 degrees understanding... know thyself.

We live the real. We are not professionally trained nor colonizer puppets. We have secrets of pyramids and hieroglyphics in our hearts and heads. We are living mathematics, demonstrating the sciences of life, manifesting true and living divine light as our way of life.

Please do not get caught on hot mics... you know the permissions are on at all times of night. Laptop keystrokes will expose you, your cell will tell, your vehicle will show you cannot navigate, your home's convenient tech will capture your every Alexa command, your temperatures, your laundry cycle, every perverted request. Your on-and-off moments are a test... it is in all places, every place, all at once. Technology abounds—friend, foe, showstopper, **watchers**.

|| "This Could be Heaven or This Could be Hell" ||

Some dance to remember; some dance with regrets.

Hate and harm are seductive devices of abusers, a shimmering light in the night. A wicked addiction straddling, a willingness to commit ill will, taking all participants prisoner, draining humanity out of the minds and hearts of the users as it distills. People plead historical racism as an alibi, saying it set all in motion, stabbing at it with steely knives... but never quite killing the beast. Where we fail is not stripping away the poison and corruption coursing through our veins, acquiescing to the ease of violent tendency, and subjugation of other humans.

Perpetrated evils claimed progress, to leapfrog onto the scene of nations instead reaped in a path of dread. We fueled our nation forward, specializing in the export of hate, bigotry, classism, and race.

Last check, bills and laws alone do not evolve thinking... an unfortunate caste system woven throughout our social structure, a hardwired frame of thinking, shall not be toppled with tokens dropped into the slots of current power dynamics hoping for a jackpot of change. Thus, these tokens can be recanted/retracted via subsequent bills, laws, and legal challenges stemming from a philosophical conformity stature of what "will be" considered acceptable. There is no shielding in consorting with those who purport to be "different."

We really need to check our history... Dred Scott is a classic tutelage for all groups fighting and aspiring for equitable representation. It is an insight into an oppressor's mindset— signed laws, challenged in court, navigating a system of things, turned by panels of judges of the land "supreme" legal authority, a rule of the majority appointed through selection by minority... So, while people celebrate temporal wins, the fight only begins against shallow hearts that are graves for conscience.

Hate and racism are addictive drugs of rulership. Welcome to the USA, a hotel where lost souls and dreams go to dwell... a primordial hell.

|| Inner Light ||

The flame that guides.

Protect your inner light that inspires uniqueness, stimulates difference of perspective, and nurtures the beauty of who you are.

The world will send gusts of winds to subdue your flame. Some winds will be cold, harsh, judgmental conformists. Others will be warm and comforting, reaffirming your strength as you blaze.

Whatever you do, shield your flame from elements that come pouring down, extinguishing rains an effort to dowse your flame. We need you in this world with us, radiating light on the path forward in hope, truth, and love.

"Your need for acceptance can make you invisible in this world.
Don't let anything stand in the way of the light that shines through this form. Risk being seen in all of your glory."
— **Jim Carrey**

|| Insist, Persist, Resist ||

Insist upon being true to your pneuma. Persist in learning to expand your capacity striving to be the best of your present self. Resist social constructs and categories that are imposed upon you. They are limited frames of mind; they do not quantify nor qualify your potential. Lastly, believe in your potential, continue to grow from within, and wisely invest your time with those who challenge you to higher degrees of thee, raising the bar repeatedly.

Remember, your best self is ever-elevating.

|| Is There a Doctor in the House? ||

The work of healing human experiences.

When you go to a medical doctor for treatment related to an ailment, at the bare minimum, you expect that doctor to engage with you in some way. You expect at least an examination— questions about "why" you are seeking assistance, "what" your symptoms are, specifics of "when" it happens/happened, and "where" you are experiencing said aliment. Subsequently, the doctor might request "labs" to get beyond verbal descriptors, gathering more data.

What if, when you scheduled a doctor's appointment, instead of receiving a scheduled time, whether virtually or in person, you automatically received a prescribed regimen? What would you think about that? Would you think the doctor performed due diligence or even cared about you as an individual? A medical doctor who did not take the time to interact, explore what you are experiencing, take your temperature, capture some vitals, examine affected areas, inquire how long you've experienced this discomfort, or understand more about your health history—that would be concerning. (minimal data collection is expected). You would more than likely think and feel this doctor is not taking the time to hear you or understand your condition nor what you are experiencing.

So, hold that thought. Swap "medical doctor" for commercialized hacks claiming to solve long-term issues related to social injustices, inequitable standards, processes, policies, laws, practices, behaviors, resources, lack of access, and minimal diverse representation in every aspect of the socio-political-business sphere, coupled to no authentic inclusion. That is what commercialized, sterile company-speak for DEI, EDI, JEDI, DEIB, etc., are. Our movement has been culturally hijacked with bolt-on initiatives by mainstream culture cockroaches who sanitize messaging to maintain status-quo power dynamics. Not to mention all the time turning a coin.

We must remain steadfast in our commitment to disrupt shallow initiatives that hand out swag with catchy phrases, cupcakes, and present dressed up poster boards as diversity. Where are the measurements? Where are the goals? How are we tracking? What are the expected deliverables, impacts, outcomes? What alternative plans are lined up to course-correct? Dig in with the Five-Whys after that.

We must stimulate change that triggers a diametric, dynamic shift toward critical inquiry and interactions, recognizing the entire human family as a peer group and neighbors. Instead, we have been hacked by slogans and peppered with jargon and unapplied group agreements and forward-facing materials that are void of substantive and visionary change. We are no longer a movement. We have been moved on.

Take care, my friends. Be strong, starting first from within.

|| Radical ||

Radical - / ˈradək(ə)l/ * *(Google search)*

    1. *relating to or affecting the fundamental nature of*

something; far-reaching or thorough.

2. *advocating or based on thorough or complete social change; representing or supporting an extreme or progressive shift in being.*

3. *a person who advocates thorough or complete reform.*

There are people presented in our lives, whether at work, events, random encounters at a store, or brief passings. They enter like a powerful flash of light, radically disrupting our thinking and vision about our perception of reality. They stir an aspect of our being we have ignored, silenced, run from, or are plain scared of. Yet, they illuminate what we did not, could not, would not, or refused to recognize and acknowledge in life: quantum vibrations of multi-dimensions worlds sensation. They disturb and disrupt in ways that we consider outrageously reckless or on no occasion dared to pursue because it was too terrifying, while awesomely inspiring.

And, before we knew it, they were gone. In their wake, we hear the thunder and rumble clap of their impact. We wonder why we did not grasp that energy, that powerful magnificence to chase splendor of the kaleidoscope. Now that they have moved on or are gone, we recognize the brilliance, grace, kindness, and majestically unspoken power they emitted. In some regards, our soul aches that we did not drop everything to chase that light beckoning us closer to our true selves.

They have transcended, busy about the work, not waiting for everyone or anyone to catch up. Their pace is and was so intense. This plane of being can only harbor so much power. Still, we feel their reverberating rumble of life, the truth amplified as they invited us to take those steps, to walk through our fears. They saw so much more beauty, majesty in each one of us. We just had not and have not realized it. They came and struck with such vividness, blinding us momentarily as we adjusted, trying to comprehend their love—love for life, for us, love of the experiences... Every aspect of it, valleys, and peaks.

They shook us from a slumber of not knowing. They showed us how magnificent life can be if we only embrace it as an experience of *Being*. Live your best life, by giving unto it, being alive.

Lightning and thunder.

|| Locked-In, Let's Roll ||

Being in a space of agitated disruption.

"Hope and fear cannot occupy the same space. Invite one to stay,"
—Maya Angelou

We are at an entry point that opens to pathways leading to various destinations. Choose wisely.

We are not satisfied with the current status quo, nor should we be. It requires courage to step forward toward something new and unknown. The potential of newness brings uncertainty and the unforeseen. We can approach it with fear in our hearts or we can approach it with hope.

Fear can be a healthy warning, telling us we must be on point, proactive versus reactive. Yet, we cannot allow fear to command our spirit—that is the antithesis of being alive. There is no time to dwell upon a multitude of possibilities... being immobilized guarantees us more of the same.

Now is the time to decide which shall rule your heart: fear or hope. Hope for something better, for something new, for change, opportunity, the truth of humanity, authentic yearning, for something we have not genuinely done to date.

Embrace the resilience of the human spirit—being thoughtful, caring, daring, vigorous, loving, and powerful.

I invite hope to stay... because I know fear leads to stagnation and death. Leave that behind; let us press forward towards the mountains of unknow moons.

Let's get it.

|| Looking at the World through a Peephole ||

Most people know peepholes limit what can be seen. Yet, they are useful especially when we only need to quickly check something on the other side. Still, we must open the door fully to see better and let someone in.

Microscopes have the power to magnify small things, from a base power of 4x, 10x, 40x, 100x. Yet, microscopes can only provide intense amplification of things within an extremely small space.

A typical piano has eighty-eight keys. The expectation when playing melodies is that we will have full access to all the keys. How would melodies sound if people were only able to use one or two keys?

The alphabet has vowels and consonants. What if certain people were not given access to vowels?

The point is that we require full access to all aspects of life to gain insight, be informed, analyze data, broaden perspectives, and better understand circumstances/situations, and life for the broader human family throughout the world. Without expanding beyond microscopic views based on limited information and tools and without full access, whatever we attempt to produce will be finite in reach.

What we see, what we can deduce from narrow contexts, will produce distorted concepts, warped assumptions, broken melodies, incoherent words. Hence, results will be completely out of step with the world around us, as well as our ability to connect with other people. We will be misunderstood and unable to fully communicate with people, ultimately limiting our comprehension of humanity...

We must open our minds to more encompassing perspectives, ideas, concepts, information, knowledge, and lived experiences—and stop looking at the world through the peepholes of social media, ignorance, hate, and racism.

|| Melancholy of the Day ||

When the good become indifferent.

"I have absolutely no pleasure in the stimulants in which I sometimes so madly indulge. It has not been in the pursuit of pleasure that I have periled life and reputation and reason. It has been the desperate attempt to escape from torturing memories, from a sense of insupportable loneliness and a dread of some strange impending doom."

—**Edgar Allan Poe**

Each day, we wake with brave aspirations to change the wrongs of our world. As night falls, the world bellows, closing in upon us, laughing at our pain to overcome that which is not right.

Please be brave, stay with us another day, my friend, each day, again and again. Because only on this side of reality can we make the difference for another day. Let us transform the world together.

Remain amongst us, my friend.

|| My Health, Not Yours ||

"To wake up every day waiting for someone to accept, validate, and to love you is a disappointing life. You have to work to do those things for yourself. You can do this by accepting who you are. By acknowledging your gifts and talents. Stop assuming that people

are better than you. Stop calling yourself names and correct the negative thoughts. Focus on the positive things in your life while you fix the broken pieces."

—Christopher Lemark[8]

Mental health is an important state of well-being in which individuals develop the ability to cope with normal stress, relate to others, and make healthy choices. The starting point is introspection and recognizing that "being perfect" is a fallacy and to be human is a learning experience every day.

There will be peaks and valleys as we travel through life. It would be a wonderful thing if we could somehow remain within the radius and summit of great experiences. Yet, we must journey forward through valleys that will challenge, push, hurt, and tear at our inner being. Again, we must have the courage to continue taking a step and then the next because "this, too, shall pass."

Not every day will we win the battle, but as students of life, we must always search our hearts to gain perspective and learn. Know that in those darkest hours, with a few more precious steps, we will reach that summit to learn another great lesson in this life. And the light of learning will warm us again so that we can reflect and radiate the beauty of that omniscient light for others to see a path forward.

|| Mental Prisons ||

Change - /CHānj/ (Google search)*

1. *the act or instance of making or becoming different.*

2. *make (someone or something) different; alter or modify.*

Prison - /ˈprizən/ (Google search)*

1. *a building in which people are legally held as a punishment*

---

[8] https://chhamh.org/founder

*"Prison is designed to break one's spirit and destroy one's resolve.
To do this, the authorities attempt to exploit every weakness,
demolish every initiative, negate all signs of individuality all with
the idea of stamping out that spark that makes each of us human
and each of us who we are".*

**—Nelson Mandela
(*Solitary*, by Albert-Woodfox)**

The greatest prisons of all are ones of the mind. Most of us live our day-to-day lives in prison. We have designed it based upon constructs that are taught and imposed by social standards. Mental prisons are designed upon dominant social norms, we are taught this right from our first breath, whether from family, friends, loved ones, or authority figures of some form over time. We adopt these mental models of "what good looks like" early on; we cannot recall when we didn't accept them. At what point in time were these shackles placed upon us? Or did we reach for them and place them upon ourselves?

Physical bondage becomes unnecessary when constraints from others impose limitations of what we think we can be, especially when accepted wholeheartedly. Mental constraints become of our own making, "a mental prison" that we accept and are terrified of breaking free from.

I am here to tell you that each of us holds the keys within to break free, to escape these mental prison cells of conformity...

When we fear questioning and accept social, political, and professional scripts and roles of being -on accepting them on face value, we accept mental bondage. We become jailers. And we view our reality through distorted lenses of systematic oppression placed upon us over time—so much so that self-imposed limitations rooted in our mentalities hamper us from what and who we truly are and can be!

Where are the keys to breaking these mental fetters? Stop accepting the restrictions that others and society tell you about who and what you should or can be. Challenge your thinking, and every time someone or some standard is cited to you on what limitations you must accept, ask "Seven Whys." It is about elevating our mentalities, shaking off the shackles of conformity, and no longer "knowing our place." That is what I mean by being disruptive... We are all valuable. Simply because someone is on an executive board, a CEO, VP, director, manager, or leadership position does not make them better. Those are roles and positions, not the quality of character and substance of who we are as human beings.

You have just as much ability, if not more, to influence the world around you. Disrupt your present reality by shifting your thinking about the narrative: social, political, and professional norms you have been taught to accept. The human family has never been one-dimensional, yet "others" throughout history have attempted to prescribe "swim lanes": roles, class, race, religion, status, etc. We must break away from these limiting beliefs and disrupt these stifling forms of bondage. We hold the keys to these mental prisons; all we must do is dare not to accept our place as defined by others.

|| Mental Warfare ||

A cage to know thy place.

Oppression is cast against us multi-dimensionally, mentally, physically, and spiritually. Physical oppression is established by force, with brutality, laws, policies, and practices geared to alienate, subdue, limit, and control what we can or cannot do. But those can be readily identified and pointed out.

Mental oppression is incorporated into how groups of people are portrayed in historical accounts (the pillager writing the narrative). This funnels mental suffocation into our educational system, exalting the oppressor over the oppressed, nurturing a mindset inclined towards submission because there always must be winners and losers. And that mentality of conqueror and conquered are stitched into every aspect of our social dynamic. This stranglehold impacts the political, business, civil, and economic spheres, thus it is the most dangerous—most dangerous because it corrupts the hearts of human beings and turns us against one another at scale.

Spiritual oppression: we are laden with the lust to have everything we want without limitations or consideration of long-term ramifications. We sell each piece and parcel of our souls to indulge unabashed desires and wants for material things and sensations.

As individuals, we can flip the table on these manacles. We can take back control by being discerning in what we feed our minds, as we become aware, hence shifting our ways of thinking, habits, and behaviors. Though mental oppression starts incredibly early, from the point of what we are taught as children, we have dominion. We have the ability to investigate, probe, and challenge information at any point in our lives to liberate our thinking.

Know that we must first believe the lie for it to influence how we view our world. We must believe we are meant to be on the rungs of a social stratum to be confined by them. We must believe we are meant to be bound to remain in servitude to oppressive ways of doing. The caste system runs deep.

Break free, my friend. We need you liberated to help topple the lies.

|| My Biases ||

Hijacked by oppressor mindset cloaked as victims.

We have witnessed it again and again, the dominant culture hijacking movements, and things born from grassroot subcultures, perverting them due to a lack of authentic experiences, attunement, or understanding based in genuine struggle or perseverance. Same deal with how social justice, DEI, EDI, DEIB, and all the other twisted, flipped acronyms commercialized with claims authority in the space of social justice, equity, diversity, inclusion, and the struggle, with a dab of belonging mixed for flavor.

Next time someone tries to call you out for being biased, though they are directly aligned with a privileged, entitled, oppressive, suppressive cultural value system and equation, just smile. Do not let them get you riled up as they try to wrap themselves in a cloak claiming reversed abuse, as if they are martyrs. We got your number. Oh, Scarlett, child, you are so gone with the wind on this one.

Look them in the eyes and share your truth, with a pleasant calming smile. Say, "You know, you are absolutely right. I do have biases, and *I am biased*"—especially now that you have so politely reminded me, 'We all have biases."

I damn sure do harbor biases.

I am biased against arrogance. Against entitlement. Racism. Superiority. Bigotry. Ignorance. Ageism. Good times allies.

I am biased against knowing my place, against using social stature to bully.

I am biased against caste systems, privileged thinking, hate.

I am biased against the suppression of diversity, thinking one group of humans is better than another.

I am biased against degrading others.

I am biased against the lie of not seeing color.

I am biased against claimed reverse victimization while aligned with distorted power dynamics.

I am biased against using marginalized cultures to support the status quo outcomes.

I am biased against falsehoods, the distortion of history.

I am biased against double standards. Hypocrisy. False saviorhood. Self-aggrandizement. Fragile identities.

I am biased against thinking change must be comfortable.

I am biased against egotistical thinking and behaviors, veiled and blatant micro-aggression, and perpetuated injustice.

In summary, I am biased against bull crap.

This ain't my first rodeo. I know it when I see it and will call it.

So, tell me what are you really Biased against?

|| Perfectionism ||

Perfectionism is a complex trait characterized by striving for flawlessness and setting exceedingly lofty standards for oneself and others. While it can be a motivator, it often leads to self-criticism, procrastination, and fear of failure. From a Gemini perspective, perfectionism is a double-edged sword (definition from Google's Gemini Advance Ai).

Perfectionism is a dogma steeped in a hierarchical system of control. It is based on arbitrary standards of expectations to be redefined repeatedly, just so we are always found wanting.

Perfectionism is the perfect lie, to set people on a futile road littered with illusions continuously seeking an arbitrary measure, a subjective mark dependent upon shifting expectations. It contrives against Peoples' potential to grow working to excel, improve, and impart learnings as they navigate various aspects of understanding. The falsehood rests on the concept of allowing others to write out the definitions, terms, and conditions as a form of rulership, disguised as leadership.

The disguise traps us into frameworks allowing others to determine and judge the outcomes. Instead of nurturing, cultivating, and empowering us to elevate to higher degrees of potential. We must stop being deceived by those who are usurping our inner light for their subpar agendas and initiatives, the result of labels they can slap upon us as inadequate, disregarding what we possess in our hearts.

Life is a learning experience, and that is real. Life is not meant to be completely wrapped up in winning or losing, conquering to dominate, nor all about success with no failures... Moreso, what life is centered upon is gaining insights from which we can learn, understand, and apply going forward on a path to become better—a better expression of you. When we get stuck on winners or losers, we ironically lose sight of being present within our lived experiences.

Our life's mission is not to prove others wrong or right because they, in turn, set the goal post. It is sincerely about expressing authentically from our core, heart, and spirit. We are not in competition with others... We are competing against multiple paths, dimensions, and versions of you, growing with each step and breath, all versions of you from within, a superposition of entanglement.

|| What do we know of Love? ||

Hate produces Hate. Violence begets Violence.

As so-called leaders' position and posture on how to leverage or market incidents of violence, let us not be distracted from the harsh truth of what we, as a nation, have stoked along the way.

We have traded intellectual curiosity for ignorant catchphrases. We have acquiesced to inciting violence towards those who counter, take an opposing stance, or hold a difference in opinion and perspective, seeking to vilify them. We no longer entertain open discourse on differences or engage in constructive debate on issues. It does not matter what side of the aisle you claim or don't; far right and the far left. We advocate against opponents in terms of hatred, and we openly express cover for people who inflict harm towards others because of their differences, labeling the bad actors "good people." All the while, depicting people we take issue with as "invaders," "un-American," "unpatriotic," "socialist," and "deserving of harm."

Our failure to embrace diverse ways of thinking, doing, speaking, living, worshipping, believing, highlights our inability to be inclusive and to treat people with dignity, respect, and compassion. We would rather exclude people than be inclusive. We choose to double down on inequities rather than be equitable, and we choose to persecute people who are different from us before we are willing to nurture and activate systems changes that afford a sense of belonging for all people. We falsely trumpet that our nation was founded upon principles of religion, while using religion as a tool and mechanism to excuse racist acts. At some point, we must shake the intoxication of this bloodlust we perpetuated. We cannot continue to direct fire towards those we deem our enemies and not expect that same fire to spread in ways beyond our control.

Hate is hate, no matter who you are. Encouraging people who commit acts of violence when directed against those with whom we disagree, then feigning innocence when others perceive violence as the only thing we respect and acknowledge, is hypocritical and reckless. The sad thing is, we are not learning from the escalation of violent acts. We will not step back to pause and consider that our methods and how we deal with those who think differently, live differently, love differently, look differently, believe differently, or worship differently may be the root cause.

No, we refuse to consider whether our words of hatred influence others' actions, even as we advocate, celebrate, nod towards, wink at, and encourage them.

No, we cannot conceive of being "wrong." Just as we refuse to acknowledge societal disparities are rooted in a discriminatory order of race, gender, sexual orientation, class, national origin, religious beliefs, education, age, physical abilities, physical characteristics, the way one loves, and so many more biases and forms of bigotry.

No, we cannot even tolerate the thought of exposing our words of encouragement along this blood trail.

No, we would rather lock in and load piling on for more violence, more ignorance, more hatred, and more loss of life. We dare not imagine openly acknowledging we are complicit in these tragic outcomes. We believe doing so somehow disgraces the entire nation. Yet, the greatest disgrace lies in denying the truth to preserve the facade of lies. That is the biggest betrayal to our nation and future generations. We cannot break the cycle with more rhetoric that incites harm.

Yet, I fear we will continue to learn nothing. We seem hell-bent and determined that this nation can only be geared as a caste system, that there is only one way of leadership: brutal rulership, through dominance, forced submittance, conformity and ultimate oppression. We are steadfast in our pursuit to strip out any aspirations towards the ideals of freedom, justice, equality, liberty, and the irrevocable truth that all people are created equal.

We cannot seem to summon the courage, moral fortitude, belief, compassion, hope, or humanity to open our minds and see where this divisive form of politics, so-called leadership and power plays are leading our nation: implosion. No, we refuse to acknowledge the obvious signs. We are seeking our own destruction, weakening ourselves from within so those who lust for ultimate power and control can lord over us all. As fools we shall not soon part from our folly.

Now I utterly understand what James Baldwin meant in the statement that there is a small number of people who genuinely love, holding the world together. I have struggled to understand those words over the years, each time I heard the recording. But now, I really do understand what it means for us.

"Love has never been a popular movement. And no one's ever wanted, really, to be free. The world is held together, really it is held together, by the love and the passion of a very few people. Otherwise, of course, you can despair. Walk down the street of any city, any afternoon, and look around you. What you've got to remember is what you're looking at is also you. Everyone you're looking at is also you. You could be that person. You could be that monster, you could be that cop. And you have to decide, in yourself, not to be."

—James Baldwin, from the documentary short "Meeting the Man: James Baldwin in Paris."

∞ About the Author

|| Shabazz A. Rah-Khem, Ph.D. ||

Dr. Rah-Khem is a thought leader and catalyst for change. His doctoral research in Organizational Behavior, with a focus on Emergent Change, illuminates the complex interactions between systems, individuals, and organizations.

Leveraging these insights and his experience in strategic planning and implementation, Dr. Rah-Khem champions social justice initiatives. He is a relentless evangelist and advocate for systemic change and innovation, to transform communities through equitable access to resources, education, economic opportunities, and political representation. His lived experiences fuel a deep commitment to bridging societal divides and empowering marginalized communities.

Dr. Rah-Khem maintains a radical optimism in humanity's collective creativity to address the dynamic challenges facing our global communities. However, he emphasizes a critical point:

"We must break the stranglehold of ignorance, hate, and racism."